J. A. Froude (1828–1894)
*The Reign of Mary Tudor*
(1860)

Eamon Duffy is Professor of The History of Christianity at The University of Cambridge and a Fellow of Magdalene College. His most recent book was *Fires of Faith: Catholic England under Mary Tudor* (Yale University Press, 2009). Two previous titles, *Faith of Our Fathers* (2004) and *Walking to Emmaus* (2006), were both published by Continuum.

## CONTINUUM HISTORIES
**The greatest narrative history writing in English**

This series is designed to attract a new generation of readers to some of the greatest narrative history ever written. Each volume includes a dramatic episode from a major work of history, prefaced with an introduction by a leading modern authority.

**Continuum Histories** demonstrate the extraordinary tradition that exists of great history writing in the English language – and that often the best stories are true stories.

Series Editor: Mark Bostridge

# The Reign
# of Mary Tudor

**Also in Continuum Histories**

William H. Prescott's *History of the Conquest of Mexico*.
Introduced and selected by J. H. Elliott

Lord Macaulay's *History of England*.
Introduced and selected by John Burrow

Edward Gibbon's *Decline and Fall of the Roman Empire*.
Introduced and selected by Tom Holland (forthcoming)

Thomas Carlyle's *The French Revolution*.
Introduced and selected by Ruth Scurr (forthcoming)

J. A. FROUDE

# The Reign
# of Mary Tudor

Introduced and selected by
**Eamon Duffy**

continuum

**Published by the Continuum International Publishing Group**

| The Tower Building | 80 Maiden Lane |
| 11 York Road | Suite 704 |
| London | New York |
| SE1 7NX | NY 10038 |

www.continuumbooks.com

First published 2009

British Library Cataloguing-in-Publication Data
A catalogue record for this book is available from the British Library.

ISBN 978-1441-18685-0

Designed and typeset by www.benstudios.co.uk
Printed and bound by the MPG Books Group

# CONTENTS

# INTRODUCTION

Great historical writing, perhaps all historical writing, holds a mirror up to two different worlds: the age it sets out to describe, and the age in which it is written. The historian aims to understand and explain the past. But the questions historians bring to the past often reflect the anxieties and preoccupations of the present. Of no great historical work is this more true than James Anthony Froude's monumental 12-volume study of *The History of England from the Fall of Wolsey to the Defeat of the Spanish Armada*, published between 1858 and 1870.[1]

Froude's intellectual career was stormy even by the contentious standards of Victorian England. Born in 1818, he was the fourth son of a stern West Country parson. His father was an old-fashioned, high and dry churchman, archdeacon of Totnes from 1820 till his death in 1859. His mother died two years after James Anthony's birth. The future historian was raised in a male-dominated household of rigid discipline and little overt affection, disapproved of at home and bullied at school. He was overshadowed by his brilliant, ebullient and egotistical eldest brother Hurrell, whose idea of toughening his timid and sickly sibling was to lower him head-first into a Devon stream and stir the mud with his hair.[2] Before his premature death from tuberculosis in 1836, Hurrell was to become one of the founding fathers of the 'Tractarian' Movement, the Oxford-based, clerical ginger group which sought to recover and promote the Catholic aspects of the Anglican tradition. The publication of Hurrell Froude's inflammatory and opinionated literary *Remains* by his friend and admirer John Henry Newman in 1838 was both a turning point in the history of the movement, and a staging post on Newman's own journey into the Roman Catholic Church.

James Anthony arrived in Oxford just months before his brother's death, and fell at once under the spell of Newman's magnetic personality. His first historical work was a life of the Saxon St Neot, which he contributed to a hagiographical series on the English saints edited by the older man. Froude was never to lose his personal reverence for Newman, 'one of the ablest of living men'[3], but he soon found himself repelled by Newman's religion, with its emphasis on the importance of dogma and the continuity of Catholic tradition. Unsettled by a *zeitgeist* in which traditional religious certainties seemed increasingly contradicted by advances in science and biblical criticism, Froude abandoned what he saw as the hot-house churchiness of Tractarianism. After much agonizing, he took refuge in a self-consciously low-church Protestantism, fiercely patriotic, deeply anti-clerical, dismissive of doctrine and ceremonial. Froude emphasized instead religion as moral goodness informed by faith in a providentialist God, known in the course of history by the individual conscience.[4] For him, the triumph of the Reformation did not lie in the replacement of a Catholic creed by a Protestant one, for Froude himself had reservations about all creeds whatever. What Henry VIII and his daughter Elizabeth had achieved, instead, was the shattering of clerical power, and the liberation of the lay conscience from ecclesiastical control and nonsensical mumbo-jumbo. In the Tractarian nostalgia for the Catholic past and, even more, in the contemporary revival in England of the Roman Catholic Church, Froude saw a mindless retreat on superstition and intellectual oppression.

Victorian England was militantly Protestant. Yet disparagement of the Reformation was common among early Victorian writers. The great Whig historian, Thomas Babington Macaulay, valued the sixteenth-century break with the Papacy as a step away from obscurantism on the road to modernity. But he saw the Reformation itself as an ignoble episode, initiated by tyranny and driven by the basest of motives:

> Elsewhere, worldliness was the tool of zeal. Here, zeal was the tool of worldliness. A King, whose character may best be described by saying that he was despotism itself personified, unprincipled ministers, a rapacious aristocracy, a servile Parliament, such were the instruments by which England was delivered from the yoke of Rome.[5]

For quite different reasons, the Tractarians also distanced themselves from the first Reformers, because they had repudiated the Catholic inheritance which the Oxford Movement now sought to reinstate. In one of the most notorious sentences in Hurrell Froude's *Remains*, James Anthony's brother declared the English Reformation to be 'a limb badly set – it must be broken again to be righted'. Newman too had cast a bleak eye on the founding fathers of Anglicanism: 'Cranmer will not stand examination', he had written in 1838, 'the English Church will yet be ashamed of conduct like his'.[6]

These jaundiced views of the Reformation and its leaders had been given formidable scholarly underpinning by the work of a learned Catholic historian, the priest John Lingard. His soberly understated ten-volume *History of England*, completed in 1830, had marshalled new material from hitherto unexploited European archives into a deeply unflattering picture of the origin and progress of Henry VIII's break with Rome.[7] Despite his suspect status as a Catholic priest, Lingard's scholarship was widely respected and, though he seldom mentioned him by name, Froude often had this influential Catholic historian firmly in his sights.

Froude's great *History* was therefore deliberately conceived as a defence of the English Reformation. It was, however, financial necessity that drove Froude to the writing of that history. In 1849 he published a lurid semi-autobiographical novel, *The Nemesis of Faith*, whose clerical hero is plagued by religious doubts, flirts with adultery and suicide, becomes a Roman Catholic and enters a monastery, but ultimately dies in despair. The scandal which erupted around this sensational novel changed the course of Froude's life. His horrified father disowned him, and he was forced to resign his Fellowship at Exeter College Oxford. To hold his Fellowship in the first place, he had been obliged to accept ordination as a deacon in the Church of England, despite his religious doubts. This unwanted clerical status now legally prevented Froude earning a living in any of the other professions. Married, and with a growing family, he settled in idyllic, if impoverished, seclusion at Plas Gwynant, near Snowdon in North Wales, in 1850. He commenced work as a jobbing journalist, writing reviews and essays for many periodicals. Froude also conceived the idea of a biography of Elizabeth I and began reading the available printed sources. As he became more absorbed, the scope of the project widened to take in the whole of the English Reformation, understood as 'a revolt against idolatry and superstition...of the laity against the clergy, and of the English nation against the papal supremacy'.[8]

Froude was fortunate in his timing. Until the early nineteenth century, the history of England had been written largely from printed sources: manuscript archives were mostly uncatalogued, difficult to locate and to gain access to, once located. Lingard had recognized the importance of going to the archives if old stereotypes were to be overthrown and had made pioneering use of manuscript material in the Vatican and other European depositories. But the bulk of the state papers for sixteenth-century England were not yet accessible to historians, the great Victorian publication of series of state papers not yet conceived.

By the time Froude came to write, however, that situation was changing. The Public Record Office had been established in Chancery Lane in London in 1838, the first step towards centralizing and opening to researchers the national archives, till then scattered in more than 50 different locations. The Deputy Keeper of the Public Records Sir Francis Palgrave had begun transcribing and calendaring the records for the reign of Henry VIII and made these transcriptions available to Froude. They provided him both with the framework for the early volumes of his history and with a sense of the sheer quantity of the treasure as yet unexplored. He moved to London to be near the sources and became a dedicated archival historian, searching out sixteenth-century papers not merely at the Public Record Office, but in great family collections like the Cecil Papers at Hatfield.[9]

For the Elizabethan volumes of his history, he would spend gruelling months in the heat, dust and uncatalogued chaos of the Spanish archives at Simancas.[10]

Froude's reliance on manuscript sources was his proudest boast as an historian. Nine-tenths of his source materials, he insisted, were manuscripts which no-one else had used. Ironically, that very claim became a favourite target of gleefully hostile reviewers. Froude worked rapidly on manuscript materials in five languages, under constant pressure of time, in atrocious conditions, too dark, too cold, too hot, often without the benefit of calendars or finding lists, and with no research assistants. Never a careful proofreader, and with no formal training in palaeography, he sometimes had to guess, as much as read, the meaning of the crabbed and blotted texts he was deciphering and he did not always guess right. In taking notes, sometimes he transcribed verbatim, sometimes he paraphrased. When reproducing his sources in print, he did not always distinguish between transcriptions and summaries. He could be sloppy and careless, and hostile readers pounced on the slips. But, considering the pioneering nature of the work and the circumstances in which it was executed, he made amazingly few major errors. More than a century on, no less an authority than the late Sir Geoffrey Elton endorsed the essential soundness of Froude's use of the English State Papers. And when the official Calendars of the State Papers relating to England in the Spanish archives were being prepared at the end of the nineteenth century, the editors found Froude's notes and transcripts a constant and reliable guide.[11]

Froude always maintained that he had come to the writing of history with the usual inherited preconceptions and prejudices, but had had them blown away by exposure to the sources themselves.[12] In fact, his immense 12-volume narrative was profoundly shaped by his own tormented religious journey and by a distinctive and rather pessimistic world view which he brought to the sources, rather than derived from them. Having shaken free of the influence of Newman, Froude had fallen under the spell of the Scottish writer and thinker Thomas Carlyle. The fascination would last a lifetime and Froude was to become Carlyle's literary executor and, more controversially, his embarrassingly frank biographer.

Carlyle's greatest work was a history of the French Revolution, and his perception of human history was volcanic, not evolutionary. The world was indeed a moral arena in which the purposes of God worked themselves out, but always unpredictably, never gradually. The vital forces of present and future erupted shatteringly through the carapace of moribund social structures and outworn creeds. Carlyle despised optimistic Whiggish theories of the inevitability of progress through constitutional development and he identified modern democracy with the rule of little people. Instead, he believed that the spirit of the age and the great forces of change manifested themselves, for good and ill, not in the rank and file, but in the world-transforming figure of the hero – titanic individuals like Socrates, Julius Caesar, Jesus, Shakespeare, Cromwell, Frederick the Great and Napoleon.[13]

Though he would not have subscribed formally to all these ideas, they had a profound influence on Froude's understanding of the sixteenth century. He shared Carlyle's distrust of the masses, accepted contemporary racial theories which emphasized the innate superiority of some human beings to others (for example, of the English over the Irish and of the white over the black races). He regarded the advent of Protestantism and the repudiation of papal authority as an immense blessing, a necessary step in the emergence of the modern world and of English values, and a prelude to future Imperial greatness. Yet he understood perfectly well that the majority of the English people in the sixteenth century would have preferred to remain Catholic, and that the Reformation was in fact imposed on the nation by Henry VIII and his daughter Elizabeth:

> I regarded the reformation as the grandest achievement in English history, yet it was equally obvious that it could never have been brought about constitutionally according to modern methods. The Reformation had been the work of two powerful sovereigns...backed by the strongest and bravest of their subjects. To the last up to the defeat of the Armada, manhood suffrage in England would at any moment have brought back the Pope.[14]

It was the power of a personal monarchy, above all of Henry VIII, therefore, which had enabled and indeed enforced the transition to a new age. Though Froude recognized that there were monstrous aspects of Henry's life and actions, his instinct was to find a 'rational' justification for them and he considered that, for his great service to his people, Henry could be forgiven much. To his Victorian contemporaries, one of the most controversial aspects of Froude's history was this willingness to justify even the most autocratic and cruel actions of Henry, provided they had advanced the cause of Reformation. He defended even the law imposing boiling alive as a punishment for poisoners, and insisted that many of Henry's victims, including his executed wives, were justly punished for real crimes. Henry's Treason Act had introduced capital punishment for those unable to acknowledge the Royal Supremacy and was loathed by both by Catholic and by Whig historians as a prime example of tyrannical government attempting mind-control. Froude would have none of it:

> There are times…when the safety of the State depends upon unity of purpose…. At such times the *salus populi* overrides all other considerations: and the maxims and laws of calmer periods for awhile consent to be suspended…I assume that the Reformation was in itself right…If this be allowed, those laws will not be found to deserve the reproach of tyranny. We shall see in them but the natural resource of a vigorous Government placed in circumstances of extreme peril.

It was indeed a matter of regret that:

> in this grand struggle for freedom, success could only be won by the aid of measures which bordered on oppression.

but when all was said and done, the Catholics themselves were natural persecutors, and so had deserved the worst that was done to them:

> here also the even hand of justice was but commending the chalice to the lips of those who had made others drink it to the dregs.[15]

In this spirit, Froude defended the executions of More and Fisher and the excruciating death by disembowelling of the

Carthusian monks of Sheen for refusing the Oath of Supremacy in 1535. He admitted their courage and personal nobility, but saw that very nobility as an anachronism, an obstacle to the necessary advance of Reformation. 'We cannot blame the Government' driven to 'so hard a necessity', since 'the future of the world could not be sacrificed to preserve the exotic graces of medieval saints'.[16] This was a defence which might of course be used to legitimate the most arbitrary actions of any authoritarian regime, as many of Froude's contemporaries were quick to point out. In the margin of these very passages, the Victorian medievalist Professor E. A. Freeman, one of Froude's most relentless reviewers, scribbled indignantly 'Bah!', 'Beast!' and 'May I live to embowel James Anthony Froude'.[17]

The necessary triumph of the reformation provided Froude's sprawling narrative with an overarching general theme. But the work itself, though written with the easy grace and eloquence of a gifted journalist, was in structural terms a loose and baggy monster. It was vast in scale, leisurely in pace, sometimes racing forward in vaulting narrative, sometimes pausing for pages at a time to unravel a single incident, often incorporating vast blocs of undigested original documentation, from private letters to entire Acts of Parliament. Froude had originally intended to take the narrative to the death of Elizabeth but, late in the 1860s, decided on the defeat of the Armada as a more dramatic end point. The message as well as the form of the book evolved as Froude's own opinions shifted in response to his materials. His treatment of the reigns of Henry, Edward and Mary were originally intended essentially as an extended prelude to his much fuller treatment of the reign of Elizabeth, which did indeed eventually occupy six of the 12 volumes of the completed work. Elizabeth, rather than Henry, was

therefore the intended hero(ine) of Froude's narrative. But
as he read his way deeper into the sources, his respect for
the Virgin Queen dwindled. Though she remained for him
a providential instrument in preserving English protestant
liberties, he came to believe 'with reluctance' that:

> the wisdom of Elizabeth was the wisdom of her
> ministers, and that her chief merit...lay in allowing her
> policy to be guided by Lord Burghley.[18]

Froude's treatment of the reign of Mary I, published in
1860, was the culmination of the six volumes which make
up the first half of the *History* as a whole. It forms a genuinely
pivotal point in the unfolding of Froude's narrative, together
with the reign of Edward forming a trough between the twin
peaks of achievement represented by Henry and Elizabeth.
For Froude, Henry was a man perfectly matched to the
historic moment. At the point at which the English people
needed to unleash their potential by striking against the
'enormous tyranny' of clerical oppression, and to cast off the
foreign interference of the popes, Henry had led their bid for
freedom. Even his personal inconsistencies, the radicalism of
his break with Rome and the (richly deserved) destruction
of the monasteries, the conservativism of his belief in the
mass, matched the mood of his people:

> As the nation moved, the King moved, leading it, but
> not outrunning it; checking those who went too fast,
> dragging forward those who lagged behind.[19]

It was Henry who had masterminded the English
Reformation, and given it its distinctively national character

and it was Henry who had established Parliament as 'the first power in the State under the Crown'.[20] And correspondingly, Elizabeth had re-established and stabilized Henry's Reformation, and had defended England from being gobbled up by a politicized European Catholicism, from papistical disloyalty within and papistical invasion from abroad. The defeat of the Armada was therefore the last act in a drama that had opened with the divorce of Henry from Catherine of Aragon.

But with the death of Henry, Froude believed, the Reformation had taken a wrong turn. A national Reformation implied 'the transfer of power...from the ignoble to the noble, from the incapable to the capable, from the ignorant to the wise'.[21] Under Edward, however, ambition, greed and selfishness had triumphed and the rule of those around the child king had poisoned English public life. Liberated from the Egyptian bondage of the papacy, the people had been led not to the promised land, but into a barren wilderness where even the manna had been stolen by the Duke of Northumberland and his cronies:

> To the Universities the Reformation had brought with it desolation. To the people of England it had brought with it misery and want. The once open hand was closed; the once open heart was hardened; the ancient loyalty of man to man was exchanged for the scuffling of selfishness; the change of faith had brought with it no increase of freedom, and less of charity. The prisons were crowded as before with sufferers for opinion, and the creed of a thousand years was made a crime by a doctrine of yesterday [22]

In these circumstances, the accession of Mary seemed a deliverance:

In the tyranny under which the nation was groaning, the moderate men of all creeds looked to the accession of Mary as to the rolling away of some bad black nightmare.[23]

In fact, however, Froude believed, what was to ensue was a winnowing, a nightmare ten times worse than the reign of Edward. But it was a salutary nightmare, which Providence would use to demonstrate beyond all doubt the blessings of Protestantism and the incompatibility of Catholicism with English liberties. If indeed the Edwardine Reformation had proved to be, in Hurrell Froude's words, 'a limb badly set', then Mary's reign had broken it again with a vengeance, so that it might be set right again under Elizabeth. For Froude, therefore, Mary's reign was a tragic drama in which the queen, misguided by bigotry, hysteria and evil counsel, would squander a nation's goodwill and doom her inherited Catholicism forever to the margins of English history. The nation had cast off clerical oppression under Henry, but the people were otherwise religiously conservative. Nobody cared for the pope, or wanted the re-establishment of the religious orders, or 'the odious domination of the clergy'. But most people, Froude thought, did want the mass, the ancient ceremonies and a celibate clergy. Mary's fatal decision to try turn the clock back behind Henry's reforms, therefore, to introduce the tyranny of heresy tribunals and the slavery of papal obedience once more, snatched defeat from the jaws of victory, and doomed her regime to ignominious failure:

Could Mary have been contented to pursue her victory no further, she would have preserved the hearts of her subjects; and the reaction, left to complete its own tendencies, would in a few years, perhaps, have accomplished in some measure her larger desires. But few sovereigns have understood less the effects of time and forbearance. She was deceived by the rapidity of her first success; she flattered herself that, difficult though it might be, she could build up again the ruined hierarchy, could compel the holders of church property to open their hands, and could reunite the country to Rome.[24]

The ensuing slide into catastrophe and monstrous injustice – the folly of the Spanish marriage, the crime of religious persecution, the humiliation of the loss of Calais – followed inexorably. For Froude, Mary's failure derived in part from her own inflexible temperament. He was by no means entirely unsympathetic to her: her courageous fidelity to her religion under Edward 'determined, downright and unaffected, cutting through official insincerities and fearless of consequences', commended her to him. Froude dwelt on the paradox that it was Mary, 'the defender of a dying superstition', rather than Edward's protestant Council, 'the patrons of liberty and right', who had then held the moral high ground.[25]

But Mary as queen was a different matter. Here her frailty as a woman and her religious bigotry united to form a literally lethal combination. The 'unhappy Queen, unloved, unlovable, yet with her parched heart thirsting for affection' pined with 'hysterical longing' for a husband who would care for her, and found instead only the icy indifference of

Philip II. Her love for him became a torture to her, and a calamity for her people:

> With a broken spirit and bewildered understanding, she turned to heaven for comfort, and instead of heaven, she saw only the false roof of her creed painted to imitate and shut out the sky.[26]

Froude dwelt on Mary's desolation after Philip's departure and her first false pregnancy: 'with stomach swollen and features shrunk and haggard, she would sit upon the floor'. And he made a direct connection between that bitter disappointment and the increasingly ferocious campaign against heresy. The queen, he thought, attributed her childlessness to supernatural causes, a divine punishment.

> And what could that crime be? The accursed thing was still in the realm. She had been raised up...for the extermination of God's enemies, and she had smitten but a few....[27]

But if Froude saw in Mary's 'hysterical' temperament one of the major causes of the cruelties and failures of her reign, he laid at least equal blame on her clerical advisers – Bishops Gardiner and Bonner, straining at the leash to revenge themselves on their Protestant enemies and, above all, on the queen's cousin, Cardinal Reginald Pole. Pole is one of the recurring villains of the first six volumes of the *History*. Educated in Italy at Henry's expense and groomed for high office in the church, Pole had bitten the hand that fed him by turning against the king after the executions of More and Fisher. His treatise against the Royal Supremacy, *De Unitate*, sent to the king in

1536, embodied for Froude the ultimate treason, for in it Pole denounced his own monarch, exalted the papacy, and called on the emperor Charles V to invade England, depose Henry, and halt the Reformation. Pole's elevation to the Cardinalate in 1536 and his attempts to organize an Imperial or French 'crusade' against Henry confirmed him in Froude's mind as a treacherous betrayer of his country.

Until Froude's *History*, Pole had in fact enjoyed a surprisingly good press from English writers, which perhaps owed something to his European stature, his Plantagenet blood and his personal virtues. But for Froude, the cardinal represented fanaticism untempered by common sense. He seems to have seen in him something of the same clerical single-mindedness which had repelled him in the Tractarian movement:

> His character was irreproachable; in all the virtues of the Catholic Church he walked, without spot or stain; and the system to which he had surrendered himself had left him of the common selfishness of mankind his enormous vanity alone. But that system had extinguished also in him the human instincts, the genial emotions by which theological theories stand especially in need to be corrected.[28]

It seems likely that recollections of Froude's own brother Hurrell were not far beneath the surface when he placed Pole in:

> a class of persons at all times numerous, in whom enthusiasm takes the place of understanding; who are men of an 'idea'; and unable to accept human things as

16

they are, are passionate loyalists, passionate churchmen, passionate revolutionists, as the accidents of their age may determine.[29]

Fanatical zeal, untempered by common sense or common humanity, was for Froude the clue to the calamities of Mary's reign. He repeatedly contrasted this hysterical lack of realism with the 'judicious latitudinarianism to which the lay statesmen of the better sort were inclining.[30] It was these pragmatic realists (above all William Cecil, Lord Burghley) who saw that England's salvation lay in a return to the wholesome rationalities of the Reformation, an outcome dependent on the accession of Mary's Protestant half-sister. Elizabeth 'was the person to whom the affections of the liberal party in England most definitely tended', not least because, though she firmly rejected Catholic superstition, she was 'opposed as decidedly to factious and dogmatic Protestantism.[31] Accordingly, the preservation of Elizabeth from the hatred of the queen and the wreckage and self-destruction of Mary's doomed regime formed an important sub-theme in Froude's narrative.

Froude's portrayal of what he saw as the increasingly self-deluded character of Mary's reign focused on the queen's false pregnancies. He positively gloated over the heightened emotion and un-English excess with which both Cardinal Pole and Queen Mary deluded themselves that their regime had a future. Froude makes much of the first encounter between cardinal and queen, when Pole, amidst much un-English weeping and kissing, had blasphemously greeted Mary with the words of Gabriel to the Virgin Mary, 'Hail Mary Full of Grace, the Lord is with thee, blessed art thou amongst women, and blessed is the fruit of thy womb'. For Froude the fundamental emptiness of Marian Catholicism was reflected in the fact that, though there were to be no fruits of Mary's womb, the queen persuaded herself and others that the baby had leaped within her at Pole's words.[32]

For Froude, not only the queen but the Marian regime in general were characterized by these doomed and insubstantial emotional excesses. They 'indulged their fancy in large expectations', Catholic enthusiasm 'flowed over in processions, in sermons, masses and *Te Deums*'.[33] The regime was full of show, but ultimately as empty within as the heartless King Philip's cynical pretence of religion:

> Whatever Philip of Spain was entering upon, whether it was a marriage or a massacre, a state intrigue or a midnight murder, his opening step was ever to seek a blessing from the holy wafer.[34]

And if unreality was one of the defining marks of the Marian regime, murderous cruelty was the other. Froude detested dogmatic Protestantism almost as much as he did Catholicism, and many of the victims of the Marian burnings were very dogmatic indeed. He nevertheless devoted a sixth of his narrative of the reign to the burnings, using material from John Foxe's *Acts and Monuments* to good effect to tug at his readers' heart strings. In the process, he offered a psychologically perceptive and persuasive rehabilitation of Cranmer, who had been disparaged both by Macaulay and by Newman. Froude devoted so much space to the burnings because he believed that they, above all else, had opened the nation's eyes to the true horrors of a Catholic regime, thereby ensuring that an otherwise conservative people would return to Protestantism under Elizabeth. The 'cruelty of the Catholic party' converted the general population to the Reformation cause 'with a rapidity like that produced by the gift of tongues on the day of Pentecost'. It was a decisive step on the emergence of English identity. The 'horrible sight' of the burnings 'worked upon the beholders as it has worked since, and will work for ever, while the English nation survives'. The martyrs alone 'broke the spell of orthodoxy, and made the establishment of the Reformation possible'.[35]

To begin with, Froude's history had a rough ride from his academic contemporaries, and most of the early reviewers fastened gleefully on the work's weaknesses and errors. But public reaction was very different, and the *History* rapidly became a best-seller. The vividness and pace of the narrative, the author's contagious excitement at his many real discoveries in the archives, the brilliance of his character-drawing, and the sheer scale and grandeur of Froude's theme, the emergence of the Protestant nation in defiance of the might of Catholic Europe, caught the mood of mid-Victorian England. Tennyson was inspired by Froude's treatment of Mary's reign to write his now neglected verse drama *Queen Mary*, which Froude understandably thought the greatest of the poet laureate's works. Gladstone, at the time embroiled in his own fierce polemic against the pope and Papal Infallibility, declared that the play and, by implication, Froude's narrative which underlay it, had 'struck a stroke for the nation'.[36] Academic recognition of Froude's achievement as an historian would come belatedly, just two years before his death, in the form of his election as Regius Professor of Modern History at Oxford in 1892.

No-one would now rely uncritically on Froude's 12 volumes for an understanding of the history of sixteenth-century England. His prejudices are too blatant, his tendency to read sixteenth-century evidence through nineteenth-century spectacles too anachronistic. But many of his fundamental emphases, above all his insistence on the central role of Henry VIII in shaping the future course of English nationhood, did in fact endure, being taken up and refined by soberer (and tamer) twentieth-century academic historians. They included the most influential Tudor historian of the first half of the twentieth century, A. F. Pollard. From the 1950s onwards, Pollard's influence gave way to that of the Cambridge historian Professor G. R. Elton. Elton departed drastically from Froude's reading of the sixteenth century by transferring Henry's central role in Tudor politics and religion to his minister Thomas Cromwell. But more recent treatments of the period have returned to Froude in reinstating the king as the chief mover and shaker, even if few historians have gone as far as Froude in putting a positive spin on Henry's every action.[37]

Less happily, Froude's treatment of Mary as an hysterical personality has also survived and has coloured accounts of the queen down to the present day.[38] And in the treatment of religion in the period Froude's influence has been even more persistent. A. G. Dickens, whose textbook on the English Reformation dominated English school and university teaching from the 1960s to the 1990s, did not depart essentially from the interpretation laid down by the great Victorian. Only recently has Froude's negative and confessionally driven assessment of the Marian regime come under critical scrutiny.[39]

Froude has to be read in bulk to appreciate the vigour and pace of his narrative writing, his mastery of evocative description, his brilliantly dramatic character sketches. The shorter selections offered here have been chosen to illustrate the main themes of Froude's handling of Mary's reign – the illusory optimism of the Catholic Restoration itself, the cruelty of the persecution of Protestants, and the nature of Cardinal Pole's influence over the queen. But the first and longest of the selections offered here includes two-thirds of Froude's long opening chapter on Mary's reign, his account of the Privy Council plot to exclude her from the succession and enthrone Jane Grey in her place, her seizure of power and the downfall of the Duke of Northumberland. All Froude's skills are on display here, not least in the merciless analysis of Northumberland's desperate last days and scaffold recantation. His aphoristic summary of the career of a bold, bad man who just missed greatness shows Froude at his most characteristic:

> In his better years Northumberland had been a faithful subject and a fearless soldier, and, with a master's hand over him, he might have lived with integrity and died with honour. Opportunity tempted his ambition – ambition betrayed him into crime – and, given over to his lower nature, he climbed to the highest round of the political ladder, to fall and perish like a craven…[40]

The selection ends with the concluding pages of Froude's treatment of the reign, a sustained and deliberate exercise in inspirational rhetoric. It reminds the reader that, although Froude repudiated his Anglican ordination and considered himself a layman, he never quite exorcized the ghost of the fervent revivalist preacher he might have become.

Eamon Duffy

## SUGGESTIONS FOR FURTHER READING

The most comprehensive modern treatment of Mary's reign, based on fresh research but sharing some of Froude's attitudes, is David Loades, *The Reign of Mary Tudor: Politics, Government and Religion in England, 1553–58* (London: Longman, 1991).

A shorter study by Robert Tittler, *The Reign of Mary I* (London: Longman, 1991), takes a more positive view of Mary's achievements.

The most readable modern biography of Mary is Linda Porter, *Mary Tudor: The First Queen* (London: Piatkus Books, 2009).

The best biography of Froude is Waldo Hilary Dunn, *James Anthony Froude: A Biography* (2 vols, Oxford: Clarendon Press, 1961–3).

G. R. Elton, 'J. A. Froude and his History of England' in *Studies in Tudor and Stuart Politics and Government: Volume 3, Papers and Reviews 1973–1981* (Cambridge: Cambridge University Press, 2003) gives a great Tudor historian's assessment of Froude's continuing scholarly value.

Basil Willey, *More Nineteenth Century Studies: A Group of Honest Doubters* (London: Chatto and Windus, 1963), pp. 106–36, deals with Froude's religious odyssey.

Eamon Duffy, *Fires of Faith: Catholic England under Mary Tudor* (London and New Haven: Yale University Press, 2009) breaks radically with Froude's interpretation to offer a more positive assessment of the religious policies of Mary's reign.

## NOTES

1. I have used the standard edition, *History of England from the Fall of Wolsey to the Defeat of the Spanish Armada*. (London: Longmans, Green and Co.,1879).

2. For Froude's career:

A. F. Pollard and William Thomas, 'Froude, James Anthony (1818–1894), historian and man of letters' in *Oxford Dictionary of National Biography* (Oxford: Oxford University Press, 2004–2007).

Herbert Paul, *The Life of Froude* (London: Pitman, 1905).

Walso Hilary Dunn, *James Anthony Froude: A Biography*, (2 vols, Oxford: Clarendon Press, 1961–3).

For appraisals of his work as a Tudor historian, in ascending order of usefulness:

A. L. Rowse, *Froude the Historian: Victorian Man of Letters* (Gloucester: Sutton Publishing Group, 1987).

G. R. Elton, 'J. A. Froude and his History of England' in *Studies in Tudor and Stuart Politics and Government: Volume 3, Papers and Reviews 1973–1981*, (Cambridge: Cambridge University Press, 2003).

J. W. Burrow, *A Liberal Descent: Victorian Historians and the English Past* (Cambridge: Cambridge University Press, 1981), pp. 231–285.

3. James Anthony Froude, *Short Studies of Great Subjects* (Second Series, London: Longmans, Green and Co., 1900), p. 101.

4. Froude's religious odyssey is described in Basil Willey, *More Nineteenth Century Studies: A Group of Honest*

*Doubters* (London: Chatto and Windus, 1963), pp. 106–36.

5. 'Hallam's Constitutional History', in *Lord Macaulay's Essays and Lays of Ancient Rome* (London: Longmans, Green and Co., 1909), p. 57.

6. Hurrell Froude, *Remains of the late Reverend Richard Hurrell Froude* (London: J. G. and F. Rivington, 1838), vol. 1, p. 433.

Peter Nockles, *The Oxford Movement in Context: Anglican High Churchmanship, 1760–1857* (Cambridge: Cambridge University Press, 1994), p.124.

7. For a sometimes over-enthusiastic assessment of Lingard's originality as an historian, Edwin Jones, *John Lingard and the Pursuit of Historical Truth* (Brighton: Sussex Academic Press, 2001).

8. Dunn, *Froude*, vol. I, p. 174.

9. Paul, *Froude*, pp. 117–8.

10. Dunn, *Froude*, vol. 2, pp. 287–94.

11. Paul, *Froude*, pp. 192–8.

12. *History*, vol. IV, p. 239.

13. On Froude's intellectual indebtedness to Carlyle, Burrow, *A Liberal Descent*, pp. 252–6.

14. Dunn, *Froude*, vol. 1, p. 202.

15. *History*, vol. II, pp. 215–7.

16. *History*, vol. II, pp. 248–55.

17. Dunn, *Froude*, vol. 2, p. 464.

18. *History*, vol. I, preface.

19. *History*, vol. IV, p. 240.

20. *History*, vol. IV, p. 242.

21. *History*, vol. V, p. 99.

22. *History*, vol. V, p. 203.

23. *History*, vol. V, p. 203.

24. *History*, vol. V, p. 257.

25. *History*, vol. V, pp. 30–31.

26. *History*, vol. V, p. 411.

27. *History*. vol. V, p. 521.

28. *History*, vol. VI, pp 99–100.

29. *History*, vol. VI, pp 99–100.

30. *History*, vol. V, p. 217: c.f. his striking summary of Elizabeth's religious scepticism at the conclusion of the *History*, 'To Elizabeth the speculations of so-called divines were but as ropes of sand and sea-slime leading to the moon, and the doctrines for which they were rending each other to pieces a dream of fools or enthusiasts....She saw through the emptiness of the forms in which religion presented itself to the world.' Vol XII, p. 506.

31. *History*, vol. V, p. 226.

32. *History*, vol. V, pp. 444–5.

33. *History*, vol. V, p. 462.

34. *History*, vol. V. p. 410.

35. *History*, vol. V, pp. 523, 558, 560.

36. Alfred Lord Tennyson, *Queen Mary* (London: Henry S. King and Co., 1875).

Hallam Tennyson, *Alfred Lord Tennyson: A Memoir by his Son* (London: MacMillan and Co., 1899), pp. 562–72.

37. For the revived emphasis on the centrality of Henry, G. R. Bernard, *The King's Reformation: Henry VII and the Remaking of the English Church* (London and New Haven: Yale University Press, 2007).

38. For example, in David Loades, *Mary Tudor: The Tragical History of the First Queen of England* (London: The National Archives, 2006).

39. A. G. Dickens, *The English Reformation* (London: Batsford, 1989). For a treatment of Mary's reign that challenges the interpretation laid down by Froude, Eamon Duffy, *Fires of Fate: Catholic England under Mary Tudor* (London and New Haven: Yale University Press, 2009).

40. *History*, vol. V, pp. 246–7.

# THE REIGN
# OF MARY TUDOR

# THE ACCESSION OF THE QUEEN
# AND THE FALL OF NORTHUMBERLAND

On the 7th of July 1553 the death of Edward VI. was ushered in with signs and wonders, as if heaven and earth were in labour with revolution. The hail lay upon the grass in the London gardens as red as blood. At Middleton Stony in Oxfordshire, anxious lips reported that a child had been born with one body, two heads, four feet and hands. About the time when the letters patent were signed there came a storm such as no living Englishman remembered. The summer evening grew black as night. Cataracts of water flooded the houses in the city and turned the streets into rivers; trees were torn up by the roots and whirled through the air, and a more awful omen – the forked lightning – struck down the steeple of the church where the heretic service had been read for the first time.

The king died a little before nine o'clock on Thursday evening. His death was made a secret; but in the same hour a courier was galloping through the twilight to Hunsdon to bid Mary mount and fly. Her plans had been for some days prepared. She had been directed to remain quiet, but to hold herself ready to be up and away at a moment's warning. The lords who were to close her in would not be at their posts, and for a few hours the roads would be open. The Howards were looking for her in Norfolk; and thither she was to ride at her best speed, proclaiming her accession as she went along, and sending out her letters calling loyal Englishmen to rise in her defence.

So Mary's secret friends had instructed her to act as her one chance. Mary, who, like all the Tudors, was most herself in the moments of greatest danger, followed a counsel boldly which agreed with her own opinion; and when Lord Robert Dudley came in the morning with a company of horse to look for her, she was far away. Relays of horses along the road, and such other precautions as could be taken without exciting suspicion, had doubtless not been overlooked.

Far different advice had been sent to her by the new ambassadors of the emperor. Scheyfne, who understood England and English habits, and who was sanguine of her success, had agreed to a course which had probably been arranged in concert with him; but on the 6th, the day of Edward's death, Renard and M. de Courieres arrived from Brussels. To Renard, accustomed to countries where governments were everything and peoples nothing, for a single woman to proclaim herself queen in the face of those who had the armed force of the kingdom in their hands, appeared like madness. Little confidence could be placed in her supposed friends, since they had wanted resolution to refuse their signatures to the instrument of her deposition. The emperor could not move; although he might wish well to her cause, the alliance of England was of vital importance to him, and he would not compromise himself with the faction whose success, notwithstanding Scheyfne's assurance, he looked upon as certain. Renard, therefore, lost not a moment in entreating the princess not to venture upon a course from which he anticipated inevitable ruin. If the nobility or the people desired to have her for queen, they would make her queen. There was no need for her to stir. The remonstrance agreed fully with the opinion of Charles himself, who replied to Renard's account of his conduct with complete approval of it. The emperor's power was no longer equal to an attitude of menace; he had been taught, by the repeated blunders of Reginald Pole, to distrust accounts of popular English sentiment; and he disbelieved entirely in the ability of Mary and her friends to cope with a conspiracy so broadly contrived, and supported by the countenance of France. But Mary was probably gone from Hunsdon before advice arrived, to which she had been lost if she had listened. She had ridden night and day without a halt for a hundred miles to Keninghal, a castle of the Howards on the Waveney river. There, in safe hands, she would try the effect of an appeal to her country. If the nation was mute, she would then escape to the Low Countries.

In London, during Friday and Saturday, the death of Edward was known and unknown. Every one talked of it as certain. Yet the Duke of Northumberland still spoke of him as living, and public business was carried on in his name. On the 8th of July the mayor and aldermen were sent for to Greenwich to sign the letters patent. From them the truth could not be concealed, but they were sworn to secrecy before they were allowed to leave the palace. The conspirators desired to have Mary under safe custody in the Tower before the mystery was published to the world, and another difficulty was not yet got over.

The novelty of a female sovereign, and the supposed constitutional objection to it, were points in favour of the alteration which Northumberland was unwilling to relinquish. The "device" had been changed in favour of Lady Jane; but Lady Jane was not to reign alone: Northumberland intended to hold the reins tight-grasped in his own hands, to keep the power in his own family, and to urge the sex of Mary as among the prominent occasions of her incapacity.

England was still to have a king, and that king was to be Guilford Dudley.

Jane Grey, eldest daughter of the Duke of Suffolk, was nearly of the same age with Edward. Edward had been precocious to a disease; the activity of his mind had been a symptom, or a cause, of the weakness of his body. Jane Grey's accomplishments were as extensive as Edward's; she had acquired a degree of learning rare in matured men, which she could use gracefully, and could permit to be seen by others without vanity or consciousness. Her character had developed with their talents. At fifteen she was learning Hebrew and could write Greek; at sixteen she corresponded with Bullinger in Latin at least equal to his own; but the matter of her letters is more striking than the language, and speaks more for her than the most elaborate panegyrics of admiring courtiers. She has left a portrait of herself drawn by her own hand; a portrait of piety, purity, and free, noble innocence, uncoloured, even to a fault, with the emotional weaknesses of humanity. While the effects of the Reformation of England had been chiefly visible in the outward dominion of scoundrels and in the eclipse of the hereditary virtues of the national character, Lady Jane Grey had lived to show that the defect was not in the reformed faith, but in the absence of all faith – that the graces of a St. Elizabeth could be rivalled by the pupil of Cranmer and Ridley. The Catholic saint had no excellence of which Jane Grey was without the promise; the distinction was in the freedom of the Protestant from the hysterical ambition for an unearthly nature, and in the presence, through a more intelligent creed, of a vigorous and practical understanding.

When married to Guilford Dudley, Jane Lady had entreated that, being herself so young, and her husband scarcely older, she might continue to reside with her mother.

Lady Northumberland had consented; and the new-made bride remained at home till a rumour went abroad that Edward was on the point of death, when she was told that she must remove to her father-in-law's house, till "God should call the king to his mercy;" her presence would then be required at the Tower, the king having appointed her to be the heir to the crown.

This was the first hint which she had received of the fortune which was in store for her. She believed it to be a jest, and took no notice of the order to change her residence, till the Duchess of Northumberland came herself to fetch her. A violent scene ensued with Lady Suffolk. At last the duchess brought in Guilford Dudley, who commanded Lady Jane, on her allegiance as a wife, to return with him; and, "not choosing to be disobedient to her husband," she consented. The duchess carried her off, and kept her for three or four days a prisoner. Afterwards she was taken to a house of the duke's at Chelsea, where she remained till Sunday, the 9th of July, when a message was brought that she was wanted immediately at Sion House, to receive an order from the king.

She went alone. There was no one at the palace when she arrived; but immediately after Northumberland came, attended by Pembroke, Northampton, Huntingdon, and Arundel. The Earl of Pembroke, as he approached, knelt to kiss her hand. Lady Northumberland and Lady Northampton entered, and the duke, as President of the Council, rose to speak.

"The king," he said, "was no more. A godly life had been followed, as a consolation to their sorrows, by a godly end, and in leaving the world he had not forgotten his duty to his subjects. His majesty had prayed on his death-bed that Almighty God would protect the realm from false opinions, and especially from his unworthy sister; he had reflected that both the Lady Mary and the Lady Elizabeth had been cut off by act of parliament from the succession as illegitimate; the Lady Mary had been disobedient to her father; she had been again disobedient to her brother; she was a capital and principal enemy of God's word; and both she and her sister were bastards born; King Henry did not intend that the crown should be worn by either of them; King Edward, therefore, had, before his death, bequeathed it to his cousin the Lady Jane; and, should the Lady Jane die without children, to her younger sister; and he had entreated the council, for their honours' sake and for the sake of the realm, to see that his will was observed."

Northumberland, as he concluded, dropped on his knees; the four lords knelt with him, and, doing homage to the Lady Jane as queen, they swore that they would keep their faith or lose their lives in her defence.

Lady Jane shook, covered her face with her hands, and fell fainting to the ground. Her first simple grief was for Edward's death; she felt it as the loss of a dearly loved brother. The weight of her own fortune was still more agitating; when she came to herself, she cried that it could not be; the crown was not for her, she could not bear it – she was not fit for it. Then, knowing nothing of the falsehoods which Northumberland had told her, she clasped her hands, and, in a revulsion of feeling, she prayed God that if the great place to which she was called was indeed justly hers, He would give her grace to govern for his service and for the welfare of his people.

So passed Sunday, the 9th of July, at Sion House. In London, the hope of first securing Mary being disappointed, the king's death had been publicly acknowledged; circulars were sent out to the sheriffs, mayors, and magistrates in the usual style, announcing the accession of Queen Jane, and the troops were sworn man by man to the new sovereign. Sir William Petre and Sir John Cheke waited on the emperor's ambassador to express a hope that the alteration in the succession would not affect the good understanding between the courts of England and Flanders. The preachers were set to work to pacify the citizens; and, if Scheyfne is to be believed, a blood cement was designed to strengthen the new throne; and Gardiner, the Duke of Norfolk, and Lord Courtenay were directed to prepare for death in three days. But Northumberland would scarcely have risked an act of gratuitous tyranny. Norfolk, being under attainder, might have been put to death without violation of the *forms* of law, by warrant from the crown; but Gardiner was uncondemned, and Courtenay had never been accused of crime.

The next day, Monday, the 10th of July, the royal barges came down the Thames from Richmond; and at three o'clock in the afternoon Lady Jane landed at the broad staircase at the Tower, as queen, in undesired splendour. A few scattered groups of spectators stood to watch the arrival; but it appeared, from their silence, that they had been brought together chiefly by curiosity. As the gates closed, the heralds-at-arms, with a company of the archers of the guard, rode into the city, and at the cross in Cheapside, Paul's Cross, and Fleet Street they proclaimed "that the Lady Mary was unlawfully begotten, and that the Lady Jane Grey was queen." The ill-humour of London was no secret, and some demonstration had been looked for in Mary's favour; but here, again, there was only silence. The heralds cried "God save the queen!" The archers waved their caps and cheered, but the crowd looked on impassively. One youth only, Gilbert Potter, whose name for those few days passed into fame's trumpet, ventured to exclaim, "The Lady Mary has the better title." Gilbert's master, one "Ninian Sanders," denounced the boy to the guard, and he was seized. Yet a misfortune, thought to be providential, in a few hours befell Ninian Sanders. Going home to his house down the river, in the July evening, he was overturned and drowned as he was shooting London Bridge in his wherry; the boatmen, who were the instruments of Providence, escaped.

Nor did the party in the Tower rest their first night there with perfect satisfaction. In the evening messengers came in from the eastern counties with news of the Lady Mary, and with letters from herself. She had written to Renard and Scheyfne to tell them that she was in good hands, and for the moment was safe. She had proclaimed herself queen. She had sent addresses to the peers, commanding them on their allegiance to come to her; and she begged the ambassadors to tell her instantly whether she might look for assistance from Flanders; on the active support of the emperor, so far as she could judge, the movements of her friends would depend.

The ambassadors sent a courier to Brussels for instructions; but, pending Charles's judgment to the contrary, they thought they had better leave Mary's appeal unanswered till they could see how events would turn. There was one rumour current indeed that she had from ten to fifteen thousand men with her; but this they could ill believe. For themselves, they expected every hour to hear that she had been taken by Lord Warwick and Lord Robert Dudley, who were gone in pursuit of her, and had been put to death.

The lords who were with the new queen were not so confident. They were in late consultation with the Duchess of Northumberland and the Duchess of Suffolk, when, after nightfall, a letter was brought in to them from Mary. The lords ordered the messenger into arrest. The seal of the packet was broken, and the letter read aloud. It was dated the day before, Sunday, July 9:

"My lords," wrote Mary, "we greet you well, and have received sure advertisement that our deceased brother the king, our late Sovereign Lord, is departed to God's mercy; which news how they be woeful to our heart He only knoweth to whose will and pleasure we must and do submit us and all our wills. But in this so lamentable a case that is, to wit, now, after his majesty's departure and death, concerning the crown and governance of this realm of England, that which hath been provided by act of parliament and the testament and last will of our dearest father, you know – the realm and the whole world knoweth. The rolls and records appear, by the authority of the king our said father, and the king our said brother, and the subjects of this realm; so that we verily trust there is no true subject that can pretend to be ignorant thereof; and of our part we have ourselves caused, and as God shall aid and strengthen us, shall cause, our right and title in this behalf to be published and proclaimed accordingly.

"And, albeit, in this so weighty a matter, it seemeth strange that the dying of our said brother upon Thursday at night last past, we hitherto had no knowledge from you thereof; yet we consider your wisdom and prudence to be such, that having eftsoons amongst you debated, pondered, and well-weighed the present case, with our estate, with your own estate, the commonwealth, and all our honours, we shall and may conceive great hope and trust, with much assurance in your loyalty and service; and therefore, for the time, we interpret and take things not for the worst; and that ye yet will, like noblemen, work the best. Nevertheless, we are not ignorant of your consultation to undo the provisions made for our preferment, nor of the great banded provisions forcible whereunto ye be assembled and prepared, by whom and to what end God and you know; and nature can fear some evil. But be it that some consideration politic, or whatsoever thing else, hath moved you thereunto; yet doubt ye not, my lords, but we can take all these your doings in gracious part, being also right ready to remit and also pardon the same, with that freely to eschew bloodshed and vengeance against all those that can or will intend the same; trusting also assuredly you will take and accept this grace and virtue in good part as appertaineth, and that we shall not be enforced to use the service of other our true subjects and friends which, in this our just and rightful cause, God, in whom our whole affiance is, shall send us.

"Whereupon, my lords, we require and charge you, and every of you, on your allegiance, which you owe to God and us, and to none other, that for our honour and the surety of our realm, only you will employ yourselves; and forthwith, upon receipt hereof, cause our right and title to the crown and government of this realm to be proclaimed in our city of London, and such other places as to your wisdom shall seem good, and as to this cause appertaineth, not failing hereof, as our very trust is in you; and this our letter, signed with our own hand, shall be your sufficient warrant."

The lords, when the letter was read to the end, looked uneasily in each other's faces. The ladies screamed, sobbed, and were carried off in hysterics. There was yet time to turn back; and had the Reformation been, as he pretended, the true concern of the Duke of Northumberland, he would have brought Mary back himself, bound by conditions which, in her present danger, she would have accepted. But Northumberland cared as little for religion as for any other good thing. He was a great criminal, throwing a stake for a crown; and treason is too conscious of its guilt to believe retreat from the first step to be possible.

Another blow was in store for him that night, before he laid his head upon his pillow. Lady Jane, knowing nothing of the letter from Mary, had retired to her apartment, when the Marquis of Winchester came in to wish her joy. He had brought the crown with him, which she had not sent for; he desired her to put it on, and see if it required alteration. She said it would do very well as it was. He then told her that, before her coronation, another crown was to be made for her husband. Lady Jane started; and it seemed as if for the first time the dreary suspicion crossed her mind that she was, after all, but the puppet of the ambition of the duke to raise his family to the throne. Winchester retired, and she sat indignant till Guilford Dudley appeared, when she told him that, young as she was, she knew that the crown of England was not a thing to be trifled with. There was no Dudley in Edward's will, and, before he could be crowned, the consent of Parliament must be first asked and obtained. The boy-husband went whining to his mother, while Jane sent for Arundel and Pembroke, and told them that it was not for her to appoint kings. She would make her husband a duke if he desired it; that was within her prerogative; but king she would not make him. As she was speaking, the Duchess of Northumberland rushed in with her son, fresh from the agitation of Mary's letter. The mother stormed; Guilford cried like a spoilt child that he would be no duke, he would be a king: and, when Jane stood firm, the duchess bade him come away, and not share the bed of an ungrateful and disobedient wife.

The first experience of royalty had brought small pleasure

with it. Dudley's kingship was set aside for the moment, and was soon forgotten in more alarming matters. To please his mother, or to pacify his vanity, he was called "Your Grace." He was allowed to preside in the council, so long as a council remained, and he dined alone – tinsel distinctions, for which the poor wretch had to pay dearly.

The next day (July 11) restored the conspirators to their courage. No authentic accounts came in of disturbances. London was still quiet; so quiet, that it was thought safe to nail Gilbert Potter by the ears in the pillory, and after sufficient suffering, to slice them off with a knife. Lord Warwick and Lord Robert were still absent, and no news had come from them – a proof that they were still in pursuit. The duke made up his mind that Mary was watching only for an opportunity to escape to Flanders; and the ships in the river, with a thousand men-at-arms on board them, were sent to watch the Essex coast, and to seize her, could they find opportunity. Meanwhile he himself penned a reply to her letter. "The Lady Jane," he said, "by the antient laws of the realm," and "by letters patent of the late king," signed by himself, and countersigned by the nobility, was rightful queen of England. The divorce of Catherine of Arragon from Henry VIII. had been prescribed by the laws of God, pronounced by the Church of England, and confirmed by act of parliament; the daughter of Catherine was, therefore, illegitimate, and could not inherit; and the duke warned her to forbear, at her peril, from molesting her lawful sovereign, or turning her people from their allegiance. If she would submit and accept the position of a subject, she should receive every reasonable attention which it was in the power of the queen to show to her.

During the day rumours of all kinds were flying, but Mary's friends in London saw no reasonable grounds for hope. Lord Robert was supposed by Renard to be on his way to the Tower with the princess as his prisoner; and if she was once within the Tower walls, all hope was over. It was not till Wednesday morning (July 12) that the duke became really alarmed. Then at once, from all sides, messengers came in with unwelcome tidings. The Dudleys had come up with Mary the day before, as she was on her way from Keninghal to Framlingham. They had dashed forward upon her escort, but their own men turned sharp round, declared for the princess, and attempted to seize them; they had been saved only by the speed of their horses. In the false calm of the two preceding days, Lord Bath had stolen across the country into Norfolk. Lord Mordaunt and Lord Wharton had sent their sons; Sir William Drury, Sir John Skelton, Sir Henry Bedingfield, and many more, had gone in the same direction. Lord Sussex had declared also for Mary; and, worse than all, Lord Derby had risen in Cheshire, and was reported to be marching south with twenty thousand men. Scarcely were these news digested, when Sir Edmund Peckham, cofferer of the household, was found to have gone off with the treasure under his charge. Sir Edward Hastings, Lord Huntingdon's brother, had called out the musters of Buckinghamshire in Mary's name, and Peckham had joined him; while Sir Peter Carew, the very hope and stay of the western Protestants, had proclaimed Mary in the towns of Devonshire.

Now, when too late, it was seen how large an error had been committed in permitting the princess's escape. But it was vain to waste time in regrets. Her hasty levies, at best, could be but rudely armed; the duke had trained troops and cannon, and, had he been free to act, with no enemies but those in the field against him, he had still the best of the game. But Suffolk and Northampton, the least able of the council, were, nevertheless, the only members of it on whom he could rely. To whom but to himself could he trust the army which must meet Mary in the field? If he led the army in person, whom could he leave in charge of London, the Tower, and Lady Jane? Winchester and Arundel knew his dilemma, and deliberately took advantage of it. The guard, when first informed that they were to take the field, refused to march. After a communication with the Marquis of Winchester, they withdrew their objections, and professed themselves willing to go. Northumberland, uneasy at their conduct, or requiring a larger force, issued a proclamation offering tenpence a day to volunteers who would go to bring in the Lady Mary. The lists were soon filled, but filled with the retainers and servants of his secret enemies.

The men being thus collected, Suffolk was first thought of to lead them, or else Lord Grey de Wilton; but Suffolk was inefficient, and his daughter could not bring herself to part with him; Grey was a good soldier, but he had been a friend of Somerset, and the duke had tried hard to involve him with Arundel and Paget in Somerset's ruin. Northampton's truth could have been depended upon, but Northampton four years before had been defeated by a mob of Norfolk peasants. Northumberland, the council said, must go himself – "there was no remedy." No man, on all accounts, could be so fit as he; "he had achieved the victory in Norfolk once already, and was so feared, that none durst lift their weapons against him:" Suffolk in his absence should command the Tower. Had the duke dared, he would have delayed; but every moment that he remained inactive added to Mary's strength, and whatever he did he must risk something. He resolved to go, and as the plot was thickening, he sent Sir Henry Dudley to Paris to entreat the king to protect Calais against Charles, should the latter move upon it in his cousin's interest.

Noailles had assured him that this and larger favours would be granted without difficulty; while, as neither Renard nor his companions had as yet acknowledged Lady Jane, and were notoriously in correspondence with Mary, the French ambassador suggested also that he would do wisely to take the initiative himself, to send Renard his passports, and commit the country to war with the emperor. Northumberland would not venture the full length to which Noailles invited him; but he sent Sir John Mason and Lord Cobham to Renard, with an intimation that the English treason laws were not to be trifled with. If he and his companions dared to meddle in matters which did not concern them, their privileges as ambassadors should not protect them from extremity of punishment.

Newmarket was chosen for the rendezvous of the army. The men were to go down in companies, in whatever way they could travel most expeditiously, with the guns and ammunition waggons. The duke himself intended to set out on Friday at dawn. In his calculations of the chances, hope still predominated – his cannon would give him the advantage in the field, and he trusted to the Protestant spirit in London to prevent a revolution in his absence. But he took the precaution of making the council entangle themselves more completely by taking out a commission under the Great Seal, as general of the army, which they were forced to sign; and before he left the Tower, he made a parting appeal to their good faith. If he believed they would betray him, he said, he could still provide for his own safety; but, as they were well aware that Lady Jane was on the throne by no will of her own, but through his influence and theirs, so he trusted her to their honours to keep the oaths which they had sworn.

"They were all in the same guilt," one of them answered; "none could excuse themselves." Arundel especially wished the duke God speed upon his way, and regretted only that he was not to accompany him to the field.

This was on Thursday evening. Northumberland slept that night at Whitehall. The following morning he rode out of London, accompanied by his four sons, Northampton, Grey, and about six hundred men. The streets were thronged with spectators, but all observed the same ominous silence with which they had received the heralds' proclamation. "The people press to see us," the duke said, "but not one saith God speed us."

The principal conspirator was now out of the way; his own particular creatures – Sir Thomas and Sir Henry Palmer, and Sir John Gates, who had commanded the Tower guard, had gone with him. Northampton was gone. The young Dudleys were gone all but Guilford. Suffolk alone remained of the faction definitely attached to the duke; and the duke was marching to the destruction which they had prepared for him. But prudence still warned those who were loyal to Mary to wait before they declared themselves; the event was still uncertain; and the disposition of the Earl of Pembroke might not yet, perhaps, have been perfectly ascertained.

Pembroke, in the black volume of appropriations, was the most deeply compromised. Pembroke, in Wilts and Somerset, where his new lands lay, was hated for his oppression of the poor, and had much to fear from a Catholic sovereign, could a Catholic sovereign obtain the reality as well as the name of power; Pembroke, so said Northumberland, had been the first to propose the conspiracy to him, while his eldest son had married Catherine Grey. But, as Northumberland's designs began to ripen, he had endeavoured to steal from the court; he was a distinguished soldier, yet he was never named to command the army which was to go against Mary; Lord Herbert's marriage was outward and nominal merely – a form, which had not yet become a reality, and never did. Although Pembroke was the first of the council to do homage to Jane, Northumberland evidently doubted him. He was acting and would continue to act for his own personal interests only. With his vast estates and vast hereditary influence in South Wales and on the Border, he could bring a larger force into the field than any other single nobleman in England; and he could purchase the secure possession of his acquisitions by a well-timed assistance to Mary as readily as by lending his strength to buttress the throne of her rival.

Of the rest of the council, Winchester and Arundel had signed the letters patent with a deliberate intention of deserting or betraying Northumberland, whenever a chance should present itself, and of carrying on their secret measures in Mary's favour with greater security. The other noblemen in the Tower perhaps imperfectly understood each other. Cranmer had taken part unwillingly with Lady Jane; but he meant to keep his promise, having once given it. Bedford had opposed the duke up to the signature, and might be supposed to adhere to his original opinion; but he was most likely hesitating, while Lord Russell had been trusted with the command of the garrison at Windsor. Sir Thomas Cheyne and Shrewsbury might be counted among Mary's friends; the latter certainly. Of the three secretaries, Cecil's opposition had put his life in jeopardy; Petre was the friend and confidant of Paget, and would act as Paget should advise; Cheke, a feeble enthusiast, was committed to the duke.

The task of bringing the council together was undertaken by Cecil. Cecil and Winchester worked on Bedford; and

Bedford made himself responsible for his son, for the troops at Windsor, and generally for the western counties. The first important step was to readmit Paget to the council. Fresh risings were reported in Northamptonshire and Lincolnshire; Sir John Williams was proclaiming Mary round Oxford; and on Friday night or Saturday morning (July 15) news came from the fleet which might be considered decisive as to the duke's prospects. The vessels, so carefully equipped, which left the Thames on the 12th, had been driven into Yarmouth Harbour by stress of weather. Sir Henry Jerningham was in the town raising men for Mary; and knowing that the crews had been pressed, and that there had been desertions among the troops before they were embarked, he ventured boldly among the ships. "Do you want our captains?" some one said to him. "Yea, marry," was the answer. "Then they shall go with you," the men shouted, "or they shall go to the bottom." Officers, sailors, troops, all declared for Queen Mary, and landed with their arms and artillery. The report was borne upon the winds; it was known in a few hours in London; it was known in the duke's army, which was now close to Cambridge, and was the signal for the premeditated mutiny. "The noblemen's tenants refused to serve their lords against Queen Mary." Northumberland sent a courier at full speed to the council for reinforcements. The courier returned "with but a slender answer."

The lords in London, however, were still under the eyes of the Tower garrison, who watched them narrowly. Their first meeting to form their plans was within the Tower walls, and Arundel said "he liked not the air." Pembroke and Cheyne attempted to escape, but failed to evade the guard; Winchester made an excuse to go to his own house, but he was sent for and brought back at midnight. Though Mary might succeed, they might still lose their own lives, which they were inclined to value.

On Sunday, the 16th, the preachers again exerted themselves. Ridley shrieked against Mary at Paul's Cross; John Knox, more wisely, at Amersham, in Buckinghamshire, foretold the approaching retribution from the giddy ways of the past years; Buckinghamshire, Catholic and Protestant, was arming to the teeth; and he was speaking at the peril of his life among the troopers of Sir Edward Hastings.

"Oh England!" cried the saddened Reformer, "now is God's wrath kindled against thee – now hath he begun to punish as he hath threatened by his true prophets and messengers. He hath taken from thee the crown of thy glory, and hath left thee without honour, and this appeareth to be only the beginning of sorrows. The heart, the tongue, the hand of one Englishman is bent against another, and division is in the realm, which is a sign of desolation to come. Oh, England, England! if thy mariners and thy governors shall consume one another, shalt not thou suffer shipwreck? Oh England, alas! these plagues are poured upon thee because thou wouldst not know the time of thy most gentle visitation."

At Cambridge, on the same day, another notable man preached – Edwin Sandys, then Protestant Vice-Chancellor of the University, and afterwards Archbishop of York. Northumberland the preceding evening brought his mutinous troops into the town. He sent for Parker, Lever, Bill, and Sandys to sup with him, and told them he required their prayers, or he and his friends were like to be "made deacons of." Sandys, the vice-chancellor, must address the university the next morning from the pulpit.

Sandys rose at three o'clock in the summer twilight, took his Bible, and prayed with closed eyes that he might open at a fitting text. His eyes, when he lifted them, were resting on the 16th of the 1st of Joshua: "The people answered Joshua, saying, All thou commandest us we will do; and whithersoever thou sendest us we will go; according as we hearkened unto Moses, so will we hearken unto thee, only the Lord thy God be with thee as he was with Moses."

The application was obvious. Edward was Moses, the duke was Joshua; and if a sermon could have saved the cause, Lady Jane would have been secure upon her throne.

But the comparison, if it held at all, held only in its least agreeable features. The deliverers of England from the Egyptian bondage of the Papacy had led the people out into a wilderness where the manna had been stolen by the leaders, and there were no tokens of a promised land. To the universities the Reformation had brought with it desolation. To the people of England it had brought misery and want. The once open hand was closed; the once open heart was hardened; the ancient loyalty of man to man was exchanged for the scuffling of selfishness; the change of faith had brought with it no increase of freedom, and less of charity. The prisons were crowded, as before, with sufferers for opinion, and the creed of a thousand years was made a crime by a doctrine of yesterday; monks and nuns wandered by hedge and highway, as missionaries of discontent, and pointed with bitter effect to the fruits of the new belief, which had been crimsoned in the blood of thousands of English peasants. The English people were not yet so much in love with wretchedness that they would set aside for the sake of it a princess whose injuries pleaded for her, whose title was affirmed by act of parliament. In the tyranny under which the nation was groaning, the moderate men of all creeds looked to the accession of Mary as to the rolling away of some bad black nightmare.

On Monday Northumberland made another effort to move forward. His troops followed him as far as Bury, and then informed him decisively that they would not bear arms against their lawful sovereign. He fell back on Cambridge, and again wrote to London for help. As a last resource, Sir Andrew Dudley, instructed, it is likely, by his brother, gathered up a hundred thousand crowns' worth of plate and jewels from the treasury in the Tower, and started for France to interest Henry – to bribe him, it was said, by a promise of Guisnes and Calais – to send an army into England. The duke foresaw, and dared the indignation of the people; but he had left himself no choice except between treason to the country or now inevitable destruction. When he called in the help of France he must have known well that his ally, with a successful army in England, would prevent indeed the accession of Mary Tudor, but as surely would tear in pieces the paper title of the present queen and snatch the crown for his own Mary, the Queen of Scots, and the bride of the Dauphin.

But the council was too quick for Dudley. A secret messenger followed or attended him to Calais, where he was arrested, the treasure recovered, and his despatches taken from him.

The counter-revolution could now be accomplished without bloodshed and without longer delay. On Wednesday the 19th July word came that the Earl of Oxford had joined Mary. A letter was written to Lord Rich admonishing him not to follow Oxford's example, but to remain true to Queen Jane, which the council were required to sign. Had they refused, they would probably have been massacred. Towards the middle of the day, Winchester, Arundel, Pembroke, Shrewsbury, Bedford, Cheyne, Paget, Mason, and Petre found means of passing the gates, and made their way to Baynard's Castle, where they sent for the mayor, the aldermen, and other great persons of the city. When they were all assembled, Arundel was the first to speak.

The country, he said, was on the brink of civil war, and if they continued to support the pretensions of Lady Jane Grey to the crown, civil war would inevitably break out. In a few more days or weeks the child would be in arms against the father, the brother against the brother; the quarrels of religion would add fury to the struggle; the French would interfere on one side, the Spaniards on the other, and in such a conflict the triumph of either party would be almost equally injurious to the honour, unity, freedom, and happiness of England. The friends of the commonwealth, in the face of so tremendous a danger, would not obstinately persist in encouraging the pretensions of a faction. It was for them where they sate to decide if there should be peace or war, and he implored them, for the sake of the country, to restore the crown to her who was their lawful sovereign.

Pembroke rose next. The words of Lord Arundel, he said, were true and good, and not to be gainsaid. What others thought he knew not; for himself, he was so convinced, that he would fight in the quarrel with any man; and if words are not enough, he cried, flashing his sword out of the scabbard, "this blade shall make Mary Queen, or I will lose my life."

Not a voice was raised for the Twelfth-day Queen, as Lady Jane was termed, in scornful pity, by Noailles. Some few persons thought that, before they took a decisive step, they should send notice to Northumberland, and give him time to secure his pardon. But it was held to be a needless stretch of consideration; Shrewsbury and Mason hastened off to communicate with Renard; while a hundred and fifty men were marched directly to the Tower gates, and the keys were demanded in the queen's name.

It is said that Suffolk was unprepared: but the goodness of his heart and the weakness of his mind alike saved him from attempting a useless resistance: the gates were opened, and the unhappy father rushed to his daughter's room. He clutched at the canopy under which she was sitting, and tore it down; she was no longer queen, he said, and such distinctions were not for one of her station. He then told her briefly of the revolt of the council. She replied that his present words were more welcome to her than those in which he had advised her to accept the crown; her reign being at an end, she asked innocently if she might leave the Tower and go home. But the Tower was a place not easy to leave, save by one route too often travelled.

Meanwhile the lords, with the mayor and the heralds, went to the Cross at Cheapside to proclaim Mary Queen. Pembroke himself stood out to read; and this time there was no reason to complain of a silent audience. He could utter but one sentence before his voice was lost in the shout of joy which thundered into the air. "God save the queen," "God save the queen," rung out from tens of thousands of throats. "God save the queen," cried Pembroke himself, when he had done, and flung up his jewelled cap and tossed his purse among the crowd. The glad news spread like lightning through London, and the pent-up hearts of the citizens poured themselves out in a torrent of exultation. Above the human cries, the long-silent church-bells clashed again into life; first began St. Paul's, where happy chance had saved them from destruction; then, one by one, every peal which had been spared caught up the sound; and through the summer evening and the summer night, and all the next day, the metal tongues from tower and steeple gave voice to England's gladness. The lords, surrounded by the shouting multitude, walked in state to St. Paul's, where the choir again sang a Te Deum, and the unused organ rolled out once more its mighty volume of music. As they came out again, at the close of the service, the apprentices were heaping piles of wood for bonfires at the cross-ways. The citizens were spreading tables in the streets, which their wives were loading with fattest capons and choicest wines; there was free feasting for all comers; and social jealousies, religious hatreds, were forgotten for the moment in the ecstasy of the common delight. Even the retainers of the Dudleys, in fear or joy, tore their badges out of their caps, and trampled on them.

At a night session of the council, a letter was written to Northumberland, which Cranmer, Suffolk, and Sir John Cheke consented to sign, ordering him in the name of Queen Mary to lay down his arms. If he complied, the lords undertook to intercede for his pardon. If he refused, they said that they would hold him as a traitor, and spend their lives in the field against him.

While a pursuivant bore the commands of the council to the duke, Arundel and Paget undertook to carry to Mary at Framlingham their petition for forgiveness, in which they declared that they had been innocent at heart of any share in the conspiracy, and had only delayed coming forward in her favour from a desire to prevent bloodshed.

The two lords immediately mounted and galloped off into the darkness, followed by thirty horse, leaving the lights of illuminated London gleaming behind them.

The duke's position was already desperate: on the 18th, before the proclamation in London, Mary had felt herself strong enough to send orders to the Mayor of Cambridge for his arrest; and, although he had as yet been personally unmolested, he was powerless in the midst of an army which was virtually in Mary's service. The news of the revolution in London first reached him by a private hand. He at once sent for Sandys, and, going with him to the market cross, he declared, after one violent clutch at his beard, that he had acted under orders from the council; the council, he understood, had changed their minds, and he would change his mind also; therefore he cried, "God save Queen Mary," and with a strained effort at a show of satisfaction, he, too, like Pembroke, threw up his cap. The queen, he said to Sandys, was a merciful woman, and there would be a general pardon. "Though the queen grant you a pardon," Sandys answered, "the lords never will; you can hope nothing from those who now rule."

It was true that he could hope nothing – the hatred of the whole nation, which before his late treasons he had brought upon himself, would clamour to the very heavens for judgment against him. An hour after the proclamation of Mary (July 20), Rouge-cross herald arrived with the lords' letter from London. An order at the same time was read to the troops informing them that they were no longer under the duke's command, and an alderman of the town then ventured to execute the queen's warrant for his arrest. Northumberland was given in charge to a guard of his own soldiers; he protested, however, that the council had sent no instructions for his detention; and in some uncertainty, or perhaps in compassion for his fate, the soldiers obeyed him once more, and let him go. It was then night. He intended to fly; but he put it off till the morning, and in the morning his chance was gone. Before he could leave his room he found himself face to face with Arundel, who, after delivering the council's letter to the queen, had hastened to Cambridge to secure him.

Northumberland, who, while innocent of crime, had faced death on land and sea like a soldier and a gentleman, flung himself at the earl's feet. "Be good to me, for the love of God," he cried; "consider I have done nothing but by the consent of you and the council." He knew what kind of consent he had extorted from the council. "My lord," said Arundel, "I am sent thither by the Queen's Majesty; and in her name I do arrest you." – "I obey, my lord," the duke replied; "yet show me mercy, knowing the case as it is." – "My lord," was the cold answer, "you should have sought for mercy sooner; I must do according to my commandment."

At the same moment Sandys was paying the penalty for his sermon. The university, in haste to purge itself of its heretical elements, met soon after sunrise to depose their vice-chancellor. Dr. Sandys, who had gone for an early stroll among the meadows to meditate on his position, hearing the congregation-bell ringing, resolved, like a brave man, to front his fortune; he walked to the senate-house, entered, and took his seat. "A rabble of Papists" instantly surrounded him. He tried to speak, but the masters of arts shouted "Traitor;" rough hands shook or dragged him from his chair: and the impatient theologian, in sudden heat, drew his dagger, and "would have done a mischief with it," had not some of his friends disarmed him. He, too, was handed over to a guard, lashed to the back of a lame horse, and carried to London.

Mary, meanwhile, notwithstanding the revolution in her favour, remained a few more days at Framlingham, either suspicious of treachery or uncertain whether there might not be another change. But she was assured rapidly that the danger was at an end by the haste with which the lords and gentlemen who were compromised sought their pardon at her feet. On the 21st and 22nd Clinton, Grey, Fitzgerald, Ormond,

Fitzwarren, Sir Henry Sidney, and Sir James Crofts presented themselves and received forgiveness. Cecil wrote, explaining his secret services, and was taken into favour. Lord Robert and Lord Ambrose Dudley, Northampton and a hundred other gentlemen – Sir Thomas Wyatt among them – who had accompanied the duke to Bury, were not so fortunate. The queen would not see them, and they were left under arrest. Ridley set out for Norfolk, also, to confess his offences; but, before he arrived at the court, he was met by a warrant for his capture, and carried back a prisoner to the Tower.

The conspiracy was crushed, and crushed, happily, without bloodshed. The inquiry into its origin, and the punishment of the guilty, could be carried out at leisure. There was one matter, however, which admitted of no delay. Mary's first anxiety, on feeling her crown secure, was the burial of her dead brother, who, through all these scenes, was still lying in his bed in his room at Greenwich. In her first letter to the Imperial ambassadors, the day after the arrival of Arundel and Paget at the court, she spoke of this as her greatest care; to their infinite alarm, she announced her intention of inaugurating her reign with Requiem and Dirige, and a mass for the repose of his soul.

Their uneasiness requires explanation.

While on matters of religion there was in England almost every variety of opinion, there was a very general consent that the queen should not marry a foreigner. The dread that Mary might form a connection with some continental prince, had formed the strongest element in Northumberland's cause; all the Catholics, except the insignificant faction who desired the restoration of the Papal authority, all the moderate Protestants, wished well to her, but wished to see her married to some English nobleman; and, while her accession was still uncertain, the general opinion had already fixed upon a husband for her in the person of her cousin Edward Courtenay, the imprisoned son of the Marquis of Exeter. The interest of the public in the long confinement of this young nobleman had invested him with all imaginary graces of mind and body. He was the grandchild of a Plantagenet, and a representative of the White Rose. He had suffered from the tyranny, and was supposed to have narrowly escaped murder at the hands of the man whom all England most hated. Nature, birth, circumstances, all seemed to point to him as the king-consort of the realm. The emperor had thought of Mary for his son; and it has been seen that the fear of such an alliance induced the French to support Northumberland. To prevent the injury which the report, if credited in England, would have done to her cause, Mary, on her first flight to Keninghal, empowered Renard to assure the council that she had no thought at all of marrying a stranger. The emperor and the bishop of Arras, in assuring Sir Philip Hoby that the French intended to strike for the Queen of Scots, declared that, for themselves they wished only to see the queen settled in her own realm, as her subjects desired; and especially they would prevent her either from attempting innovations in religion without their consent, or from marrying against their approbation.

But the emperor's disinterestedness was only the result of his despondency. While the crisis lasted, neither Charles nor Henry of France saw their way to a distinct course of action. Charles, on the 20th of July, ignorant of the events in London, had written to Renard, despairing of Mary's success. Jane Grey he would not recognise; the Queen of Scots, he thought, would shortly be on the English throne. Henry, considering, at any rate, that he might catch something in troubled waters, volunteered to Lord William Howard, in professed compliance with the demands of Northumberland, to garrison Guisnes and Calais for him. Howard replied that the French might come to Calais if they desired, but their reception might not be to their taste. The revolution of the 19th altered the aspect of the situation both at the courts of Paris and of Brussels. The accession of Mary would be no injury to France, provided she could be married in England; and Henry at once instructed Noailles to congratulate the council on her accession. Noailles himself indeed considered, that, should she take Courtenay for a husband, the change might, after all, be to their advantage. The emperor, on the other hand, began to think again of his original scheme. Knowing that the English were sincere in their detestation of the Papacy, and imperfectly comprehending the insular distinction between general attachment to Catholic tradition and indifference to Catholic unity, he supposed that the country really was, on the whole, determined in its adherence to the reformed opinions. But the political alliance was still of infinite importance to him; and therefore he was anxious beyond everything that the princess whom he intended to persuade to break her word about her marriage should be discreet and conciliatory about religion. He lost not a moment, after hearing that she was proclaimed queen, in sending her his congratulations; but he sent with them an earnest admonition to be cautious; to be content with the free exercise for herself of her own creed, to take no step whatever without the sanction of parliament, and to listen to no one who would advise her, of her own authority, to set aside the Act of Uniformity. Her first duty was to provide for the quiet of the realm; and she must endeavour, by prudence and moderation, to give reasonable satisfaction to her subjects of all opinions. Above all things, let her remember to be a good Englishwoman (*bonne Anglaise*).

It was, in consequence, with no light anxiety that Renard learnt from Mary her intention of commencing her reign with an act which was so far at variance with the emperor's advice, and which would at once display the colours of a party. To give the late king a public funeral with a ceremonial forbidden by the law, would be a strain of the prerogative which could not fail to create jealousy even among those to whom the difference between a Latin mass and an English service was not absolutely vital; and the judicious latitudinarianism to which the lay statesmen of the better sort were inclining, would make them dread the appearance of a disposition that would encourage the revolutionists. She owed her crown to the Protestants as well as to the Catholics. If she broke the law to please the prejudices of the latter, Renard was warned that her present popularity would not be of long continuance.

Yet, as the ambassador trembled to know, a carelessness of consequences and an obstinate perseverance in a course which she believed to be right were the principal features in Mary's character. He wrote to her while she was still at Framlingham, using every argument which ought, as he considered, to prevail. He reminded her of the long and unavailing struggle of the emperor to bring back Germany out of heresy, where the obstinacy of the Romanists had been as mischievous to him as the fanaticism of the Lutherans. "Her duty to God was of course the first thing to be considered; but at such a time prudence was a part of that duty. The Protestant heresies had taken a hold deep and powerful upon her subjects. In London alone there were fifteen thousand French, Flemish, and German refugees, most of them headstrong and ungovernable enthusiasts. The country dreaded any fresh convulsions, and her majesty should remember that she had instructed him to tell the council that she was suspected unjustly, and had no thought of interfering with the existing settlement of the realm."

With all his efforts, however, Renard could but bring the queen to consent to a few days' delay; and fearing that she would return to her purpose, he sent to the emperor a copy of his letter, which he urged him to follow up. Charles on the 29th replied again, lauding the ambassador's caution, and suggesting an argument more likely to weigh with his cousin than the soundest considerations of public policy. Edward had lived and died in heresy, and the Catholic services were intended only for the faithful sons of the Church. He desired Renard to remind her that those who had been her most valuable friends were known to hold opinions far from orthodox; and he once more implored her to be guided by parliament, and to take care that the parliament was free. She had asked whether she should imitate Northumberland and nominate the members of the House of Commons. He cautioned her against so dangerous an example; he advised her to let the counties and towns send deputies of their own choice; and if the writs were sent into Cornwall and the northern counties, which had remained most constant to the Catholic religion, these places might be expected to return persons who would support her own sentiments.

If the emperor had been equally earnest in urging Mary to consult the wishes of her subjects on her marriage, he would have been a truer friend to her than he proved to be. But prudential arguments produced no effect on the eager queen; Renard had warned her not to resist Northumberland; she had acted on her own judgment, and Northumberland was a prisoner, and she was on the throne. By her own will she was confident that she could equally well restore the mass, and in good time the pope's authority. The religious objection to the funeral was more telling, and on this point she hesitated. Meantime she began to move slowly towards London, and at the end of the month the reached her old house of Newhall in Essex, where she rested till the preparations were complete for her entry into the city.

The first point on which she had now to make up her mind concerned the persons with whom she was to carry on the government. The emperor was again clear in his advice, which here she found herself obliged to follow. She was forced to leave undisturbed in their authorities such of her brother's late ministers as had contributed to the revolution in her favour. Derby, Sussex, Bath, Oxford, who had hurried to her support at Framlingham, were her loyal subjects, whom she could afford to neglect, because she could depend upon their fidelity. Pembroke and Winchester, Arundel and Shrewsbury, Bedford, Cobham, Cheyne, Petre, too powerful to affront, too uncertain to be trusted as subjects, she could only attach to herself by maintaining in their offices and emoluments. She would restore the Duke of Norfolk to the council; Gardiner should hold office again; and she could rely on the good faith of Paget, the ablest, as well as the most honest, of all the professional statesmen. But Norfolk was old, and the latitudinarian Paget and the bigoted Gardiner bore each other no good will; so that, when the queen had leisure to contemplate her position, it did not promise to be an easy one. She would have to govern with the assistance of men who were gorged with the spoils of the church, suspected of heresy, and at best indifferent to religion.

In Mary's absence, the lords in London carried on the

government as they could on their own responsibility. On the 21st Courtenay was released from the Tower. Gardiner was offered liberty, but he waited to accept it from the queen's own hand. He rejoined the council, however, and on the first or second day of his return to the board, he agitated their deliberations by requiring the restoration of his house in Southwark, which had been appropriated to the Marquis of Northampton, and by reminding Pembroke that he was in possession of estates which had been stolen from the See of Winchester.

On the 25th Northumberland and Lord Ambrose Dudley were brought in from Cambridge, escorted by Grey and Arundel, with four hundred of the guard. Detachments of troops were posted all along the streets from Bishopsgate, where the duke would enter, to the Tower, to prevent the mob from tearing him in pieces. It was but twelve days since he had ridden out from that gate in the splendour of his power; he was now assailed from all sides with yells and execrations; bareheaded, with cap in hand, he bowed to the crowd as he rode on, as if to win some compassion from them; but so recent a humility could find no favour. His scarlet cloak was plucked from his back; the only sounds which greeted his ears were, "Traitor, traitor, death to the traitor!" He hid his face, sick at heart with shame, and Lord Ambrose, at the gate of the Tower, was seen to burst into tears. Edwin Sandys, Northampton, Ridley, Lord Robert Dudley, the offending judges Cholmley and Montague, with many others, followed in the few next days. Montague had protested to the queen that he had acted only under compulsion, but his excuses were not fully received. Lady Northumberland went to Newhall to beg for mercy for her sons, but Mary refused to admit her.

In general, however, there was no desire to press hard upon the prisoners. Few had been guilty in the first degree; in the second degree so many were guilty, that all could not be punished, and to make exceptions would be unjust and invidious. The emperor recommended a general pardon, from which the principal offenders only should be excluded, and Mary herself was as little inclined to harshness. Her present desire was to forget all that had passed, and take possession of her power for the objects nearest to her heart. Her chief embarrassment for the moment was from the overloyalty of her subjects. The old-fashioned lords and country gentlemen who had attended her with their retainers from Norfolk, remained encamped round Newhall, unable to persuade themselves that they could leave her with safety in the midst of the men who had been the ministers of the usurpation.

Her closest confidence the queen reserved for Renard. On the 28th of July she sent for him at midnight. On the 2nd of August he was again with her, and the chief subject of her thoughts was still the funeral. "She could not have her brother committed to the ground like a dog," she said. While her fortunes were uncertain, she allowed Renard to promise for her that she would make no changes in religion, but "she had now told the lords distinctly that she would not recognise any of the laws which had been passed in the minority, and she intended to act boldly; timidity would only encourage the people to be insolent;" "the lords were all quarrelling among themselves, and accusing one another; she could not learn the truth on any point of the late conspiracy; she did not know who were guilty or who were innocent; and, amidst the distracted advices which were urged upon her, she could not tell whether she could safely venture to London or not; but outward acquiescence in the course which she chose to follow she believed that she could compel, and she would govern as God should direct her. The emperor, she added, had written to her about her marriage, not specifying any particular person, but desiring her to think upon the subject. She had never desired to marry while princess, nor did she desire it now; but if it were for the interests of the church, she would do whatever he might advise."

On this last point Renard knew more of the emperor's intentions than Mary, and was discreetly silent; on other point he used his influence wisely. He constrained her, with Charles's arguments, to relinquish her burial scheme. "Edward, as a heretic, should have a heretic funeral at Westminster Abbey; she need not be present, and might herself have a mass said for him in the Tower. As to removing to London, in his opinion she had better go thither at once, take possession of her throne, and send Northumberland to trial. Her brother's body ought to be examined also, that it might be ascertained whether he had been poisoned; and if poisoned, by whom and for what purpose."

Mary rarely paused upon a resolution. Making up her mind that, as Renard said, it would be better for her to go to London, she set out thither the following day, Thursday, the 3rd of August. Excitement lent to her hard features an expression almost of beauty, as she rode in the midst of a splendid cavalcade of knights and nobles. Elizabeth, escorted by two thousand horse and a retinue of ladies, was waiting to receive her outside the gates. The first in her congratulations, after the proclamation, yet fearful of giving offence, Elizabeth had written to ask if it was the queen's pleasure that she should appear in mourning; but the queen would have no mourning, nor would have others wear it in her presence. The sombre colours which of late years had clouded the court were to be banished at once and for ever; and with the dark colours, it seemed for a time as if old dislikes and suspicions were at the same time to pass away. The sisters embraced; the queen was warm and affectionate, kissing all the ladies in Elizabeth's train; and side by side the daughters of Henry VIII. rode through Aldgate at seven in the evening, amidst the shouts of the people, the thunder of cannon, and pealing of church bells. At the Tower gates the old Duke of Norfolk, Gardiner, Courtenay, and the Duchess of Somerset were seen kneeling as Mary approached. "These are my prisoners," she said as she alighted from her horse, and stooped and kissed them. Charmed by the enthusiastic reception and by the pleasant disappointment of her anxieties, she could find no room for hard thoughts of any one; so far was she softened, Renard wrote, that she could hardly be brought to consent to the necessary execution of justice. Against Northumberland himself she had no feeling of vindictiveness, and was chiefly anxious that he should be attended by a confessor; Northampton was certainly to be pardoned; Suffolk was already free; Northumberland should be spared, if possible; and, as to Lady Jane, justice forbade, she said, that an innocent girl should suffer for the crimes of others.

The emperor had recommended mercy; but he had not advised a general indemnity, as Renard made haste to urge. The imperialist conception of clemency differed from the queen's; and the same timidity which had first made the ambassadors too prudent, now took the form of measured cruelty. Renard entreated that Lady Jane should not be spared; "conspirators required to be taught that for the principals in treason there was but one punishment; the duke must die, and the rival queen and her husband must die with him." "We set before her" – Renard's own hand is the witness against him – "the examples of Maximus and his son Victor, both executed by the Emperor Theodosius; Maximus, because he had usurped the purple; Victor, because, as the intended heir of his father, he might have been an occasion of danger had he lived."

Looking also, as Renard was already doing, on the scenes which were around him, chiefly or solely as they might affect the interests of his master's son, he had been nervously struck by the entourage which surrounded Elizabeth and the popularity which she, as well as the queen, was evidently enjoying.

Elizabeth, now passing into womanhood, was the person to whom the affections of the liberal party in England most definitely tended. She was the heir-presumptive to the crown; in matters of religion she was opposed to the mass, and opposed as decidedly to factious and dogmatic Protestantism; while from the caution with which she had kept aloof from political entanglements, it was clear that her brilliant intellectual abilities were not her only or her most formidable gifts. Already she shared the favour of the people with the queen. Let Mary offend them (and in the intended marriage offence would unquestionably have to be given), their entire hearts might be transferred to her. The public finger had pointed to Courtenay as the husband which England desired for the queen. When Courtenay should be set aside by Mary, he might be accepted by Elizabeth; and Elizabeth, it was rumoured, looked upon him with an eye of favour. On all accounts, therefore, Elizabeth was dangerous. She was a figure on the stage whom Renard would gladly see removed; and a week or two later he bid Mary look to her, watch her, and catch her tripping if good fortune would so permit: "it was better to prevent than to be prevented."

The queen did not close her ears to these evil whispers; but for the first few days after she came to the Tower her thoughts were chiefly occupied with religion, and her first active step was to release and to restore to their sees the deprived and imprisoned bishops. The first week in August, Ponet, by royal order, was ejected from Winchester, Ridley from London, and Scory from Chichester. The See of Durham was reconstituted. Tunstal, Day, and Heath were set at liberty, and returned to their dioceses. The Bishop of Ely was deposed from the chancellorship, and the seals were given to Gardiner. "On the 5th of August," says the *Grey Friars' Chronicle*, "at seven o'clock at night, Edmond Bonner came home from the Marshalsea like a bishop, and all the people by the wayside bade him welcome home, both man and woman, and as many of the women as might kissed him; and so he came to Paul's, and knelt on the steps, and said his prayers, and the people rang the bells for joy."

While Mary was repairing acts of injustice, Gardiner, with Sir William Petre, was looking into the public accounts. The debts of the late government had been reduced, the currency unconsidered, to £190,000. A doubt had been raised whether, after the attempt to set aside the succession, the queen was bound to take the responsibility of these obligations, but Mary preferred honour to convenience; she promised to pay everything as soon as possible. Further, there remain, partly in Gardiner's hand, a number of hasty notes, written evidently in these same first weeks of Mary's reign, which speak nobly for the intentions with which both Mary and himself were setting generally to work. The expenses of the household were to be reduced to the scale of Henry VII., or the early years of Henry VIII.; the garrisons at Berwick and Calais were to be placed on a more economical footing, the navy reduced, the irregular guard dismissed or diminished. Bribery was to be put an end to in the courts of Westminster, at quarter sessions, and among justices of the peace; "the laws were to be restored to their authority without suffering any matters to be ordered otherwise than as the laws should appoint." These first essentials having been attended to, the famous or infamous book of sales, grants, and exchanges of the crown lands was to be looked into; the impropriation of benefices was to cease, and decency to be restored to the parish churches, where the grooms and gamekeepers should give way to competent ministers; economy, order, justice, and reverence were to heal the canker of profligate profanity which had eaten too long into the moral life of England.

In happier times Mary might have been a worthy queen, and Gardiner an illustrious minister; but the fatal superstition which confounded religion with orthodox opinion was too strong for both of them.

Edward's body was meanwhile examined. The physicians reported that without doubt he had died of poison, and there was a thought of indicting the Duke of Northumberland for his murder: but it was relinquished on further inquiry; the poison, if the physicians were right, must have been administered by negligence or accident. The corpse was then buried (August 6) with the forms of the Church of England at Westminster Abbey; the Archbishop of Canterbury, who had so far been left at liberty, read the service; it was the last and saddest function of his public ministry which he was destined to perform. Simultaneously, as Mary had determined, requiems were chanted in the Tower Chapel; and Gardiner, in the presence of the queen and four hundred persons, sung the mass for the dead with much solemnity. The ceremony was, however, injured by a misfortune;

after the gospel the incense was carried round, and the chaplain who bore it was married; Doctor Weston, who was afterwards deprived of the deanery of Windsor for adultery, darted forward and snatched the censer out of the chaplain's hand. "Shamest thou not to do thine office," he said, "having a wife, as thou hast? The queen will not be censed by such as thou." Nor was scandal the worst part of it. Elizabeth had been requested to attend, and had refused; angry murmurs and curses against the Bishop of Winchester were heard among the yeomen of the guard; while the queen made no secret of her desire that the example which she had set should be imitated. Renard trembled for the consequences; Noailles anticipated a civil war; twenty thousand men, the latter said, would lose their lives before England would be cured of heresy; yet Mary had made a beginning, and as she had begun she was resolved that others should continue.

In the Tower she felt her actions under restraint. She was still surrounded by thousands of armed men, the levies of Derby and Hastings, the retainers of Pembroke and Arundel and Bedford; the council were spies upon her actions; the sentinels at the gates were a check upon her visitors. She could receive no one whose business with her was not made public to the lords, and whose reception they were not pleased to sanction; even Renard was for a time excluded from her, and in her anxiety to see him she suggested that he might come to her in disguise. Such a thraldom was irksome and inconvenient. She had broken the promise which Renard had been allowed to make for her about religion; she had been troubled, it is easy to believe, with remonstrances, to which she was not likely to have answered with temper; Pembroke absented himself from the presence; he was required to retire and to reduce the number of his followers; the quarrels which began while the queen was at Newhall broke out with worse violence than ever; Lord Derby complained to Renard that those who had saved her crown were treated with neglect, while men like Arundel, Bedford, and Pembroke, who had been parties to the treasons against her, remained in power; Lord Russell was soon after placed under arrest; Pembroke and Winchester were ordered to keep their houses, and the court was distracted with suspicion, discord, and uncertainty.

From such a scene Mary desired to escape to some place where she could be at least mistress of her own movements; her impatience was quickened by a riot at St. Bartholomew's, where a priest attempted to say mass; and on Saturday, the 12th of August, she removed to Richmond. Her absence encouraged the insubordination of the people. On Sunday, the 13th, another priest was attacked at the altar; the vestments were torn from his back, and the chalice snatched from his hands. Bourne, whom the queen had appointed her chaplain, preached at Paul's Cross. A crowd of refugees and English fanatics had collected round the pulpit; and when he spoke something in praise of Bonner, and said that he had been unjustly imprisoned, yells rose of "Papist, Papist! Tear him down!" A dagger was hurled at the preacher, swords were drawn, the mayor attempted to interfere, but he could not make his way through the dense mass of the rioters; and Bourne would have paid for his rashness with his life had not Courtenay, who was a popular favourite, with his mother, the Marchioness of Exeter, thrown themselves on the pulpit steps, while Bradford sprung to his side, and kept the people back till he could be carried off.

But the danger did not end there. The Protestant orators sounded the alarm through London. Meetings were held, and inflammatory placards were scattered about the streets. If religion was to be tampered with, men were heard to say, it was better at once to fetch Northumberland from the Tower.

Uncertain on whom she could rely, Mary sent for Renard (August 16), who could only repeat his former cautions, and appeal to what had occurred in justification of them. He undertook to pacify Lord Derby; but in the necessity to which she was so soon reduced of appealing to him, a foreigner, in her emergencies, he made her feel that she could not carry things with so high a hand. She had a rival in the Queen of Scots, beyond her domestic enemies, whom her wisdom ought to fear; she would ruin herself if she flew in the face of her subjects; and he prevailed so far with her that she promised to take no further steps till the meeting of parliament. After a consultation with the mayor, she drew up a hasty proclamation, granting universal toleration till further orders, forbidding her Protestant and Catholic subjects to interrupt each other's services, and prohibiting at the same time all preaching on either side without licence from herself.

Being on the spot, the ambassador took the opportunity of again trying Mary's disposition upon the marriage question. His hopes had waned since her arrival in London; he had spoken to Paget, who agreed that an alliance with the Prince of Spain was the most splendid which the queen could hope for; but the time was inopportune, and the people were intensely hostile. The exigencies of the position, he thought, might oblige the queen to yield to wishes which she could not oppose, and accept Lord Courtenay; or possibly her own inclination might set in the same direction; or, again, she might wish to renew her early engagement with the emperor himself. The same uncertainty had been felt at Brussels; the Bishop of Arras, therefore, had charged Renard to feel his way carefully and make no blunder. If the queen inclined to the emperor, he might speak of Philip as more eligible; if she fancied Courtenay, it would be useless to interfere – she would only resent his opposition. Renard obeyed his instructions, and the result was reassuring. When the ambassador mentioned the word "marriage," the queen began to smile significantly, not once, but many times; she plainly liked the topic: plainly, also, her thoughts were not turning in the direction of any English husband; she spoke of her rank, and of her unwillingness to condescend to a subject; Courtenay, the sole remaining representative of the White Rose except the Poles, was the only Englishman who could in any way be thought suitable for her; but she said that she expected the emperor to provide a consort for her, and that, being a woman, she could not make the first advances. Renard satisfied himself from her manner that, if the Prince of Spain was proposed, the offer would be most entirely welcome.

The trials of the conspirators were now resolved upon. The queen was determined to spare Lady Jane Grey, in spite of all which Renard could urge; but the state of London showed that the punishment of the really guilty could no longer be safely delayed. On this point all parties in the council were agreed. On Friday, the 18th of August, therefore, a court of peers was formed in Westminster Hall, with the aged Duke of Norfolk for High Steward, to try John Dudley Duke of Northumberland, the Earl of Warwick, and the Marquis of Northampton for high treason. Forty-four years before, as the curious remarked, the father of Norfolk had sat on the commission which tried the father of Northumberland for the same crime.

The indictments charged the prisoners with levying war against their lawful sovereign. Northumberland, who was called first to the bar, pleaded guilty of the acts which were laid against him, but he submitted two points to the consideration of the court.

1. Whether, having taken the field with a warrant under the Great Seal, he could be lawfully accused of treason.

2. Whether those peers from whom he had received his commission, and by whose letters he had been directed in what he had done, could sit upon his trial as his judges.

The Great Seal, he was answered briefly, was the seal of a usurper, and could convey no warrant to him. If the lords were as guilty as he said, yet, "so long as no attainder was on record against them, they were persons able in law to pass upon any trial, and not to be challenged but at the prince's pleasure."

The duke bowed and was silent.

Northampton and Warwick came next, and, like Northumberland, confessed to the indictment. Northampton, however, pleaded in his defence, that he had held no public office during the crisis; that he had not been present at the making of Edward's device, and had been amusing himself hunting in the country. Warwick, with proud sadness, said merely, that he had followed his father, and would share his father's fortunes; if his property was confiscated, he hoped that his debts would be paid.

But Northampton had indisputably been in the field with the army, and, as his judges perfectly well knew, had been, with Suffolk, the Duke's uniform supporter in his most extreme measures; the queen had resolved to pardon him; but the court could not recognise his excuse. Norfolk rose, in a few words pronounced the usual sentence, and broke his wand; the cold glimmering edge of the Tower axe was turned towards the prisoners, and the peers rose. Northumberland, before he was led away, fell upon his knees; his children were young, he said, and had acted under orders from himself; to them let the queen show mercy; for himself he had his peace to make with Heaven; he entreated for a few days of life, and the assistance of a confessor; if two of the council would come to confer with him, he had important secrets of state to communicate; and, finally, he begged that he might die by the axe like a nobleman.

On the 19th, Sir John and Sir Henry Gates, Sir Andrew Dudley, and Sir Thomas Palmer were tried before a special commission. Dudley had gone with the treasonable message to France; the three others were the boldest and most unscrupulous of the Duke's partisans, while Palmer was also especially hated for his share in the death of Somerset. These four also pleaded guilty, and were sentenced, Palmer only scornfully telling the commissioners that they were traitors as well as he, and worse than he.

Seven had been condemned; three only, the duke, Sir John Gates, and Palmer, were to suffer.

Crime alone makes death terrible: in the long list of victims whose bloody end, at stake or scaffold, the historian of England in the sixteenth century has to relate, two only showed signs of cowardice, and one of those was a soldier and a nobleman, who, in a moment of extreme peril, four years before, had kissed swords with his comrades, and had sworn to conquer the insurgents at Norwich, or die with honour.

The Duke of Northumberland, who since that time had lived very emphatically without God in the world, had not lived without religion. He had affected religion, talked about religion, played with religion, till fools and flatterers had told him that he was a saint; and now, in his extreme need, he found that he had trifled with forms and words, till they had grown into a hideous hypocrisy. The Infinite of death was opening at his feet, and he had no faith, no hope, no conviction, but only a blank and awful horror, and perhaps he felt that there was nothing left for him but to fling himself back in agony into the open arms of superstition. He had asked to speak with some member of the council; he had asked for a confessor. In Gardiner, Bishop of Winchester, he found both.

After the sentence Gardiner visited him in the Tower, where he poured out his miserable story; he was a Catholic, he said, he always had been a Catholic; he had believed nothing of all the doctrines for which he had pretended to be so zealous under Edward. "Alas!" he cried, "is there no help for me?" "Let me live but a little longer to do penance for my many sins." Gardiner's heart was softened at the humiliating spectacle; he would speak to the queen, he said, and he did speak, not wholly without success; he may have judged rightly, that the living penitence of the Joshua of the Protestants would have been more useful to the church than his death. Already Mary had expressed a wish that, if possible, the wretched man should be spared; and he would have been allowed to live, except for the reiterated protests of Renard in his own name and in the emperor's.

It was decided at last that he should die; and a priest was assigned him to prepare his soul. Doctor Watts or Watson, the same man whom Cranmer long ago had set in the stocks at Canterbury, took charge of Palmer and the rest – to them, as rough soldiers, spiritual consolation from a priest of any decent creed was welcome.

The executions were fixed originally for Monday, the 21st; but the duke's conversion was a triumph to the Catholic cause too important not to be dwelt upon a little longer.

Neither Northampton, Warwick, Andrew Dudley, or Sir Henry Gates were aware that they were to be respited, and, as all alike availed themselves of the services of a confessor and the forms of the Catholic faith, their compliance could be made an instrument of a public and edifying lesson. The lives of those who were to suffer were prolonged for twenty-four hours. On Monday morning "certain of the citizens of London" were requested to be in attendance at the Tower chapel, where Northumberland, Northampton, Dudley, Henry Gates, and Palmer were brought in; and, "first kneeling down, every one of them, upon his knees, they heard mass, saying devoutedly, with the bishop, every one of them, *Confiteor.*"

"After the mass was done, the duke rose up, and looked back upon my lord marquis, and came unto him, asking them all forgiveness, the one after the other, upon their knees, one to another; and the one did heartily forgive the other. And then they came, every one of them, before the altar, every one of them kneeling, and confessing to the bishop that they were the same men in the faith according as they had confessed to him before, and that they all would die in the Catholic faith." When they had all received the sacrament, they rose and turned to the people, and the duke said:

"Truly, good people, I profess here before you all, that I have received the sacrament according to the true Catholic faith: and the plague that is upon the realm and upon us now is that we have erred from the faith these sixteen years; and this I protest unto you all from the bottom of my heart."

Northampton, with the rest, "did affirm the same with weeping tears."

Among the spectators were observed the sons of the Duke of Somerset.

In exhibiting to the world the humiliation of the professors of the gospel, the Catholic party enjoyed a pardonable triumph. Northumberland, in playing a part in the pageant, was hoping to save his wretched life. When it was over he wrote (August 22) a passionate appeal to Arundel.

"Alas, my lord," he said, "is my crime so heinous as no redemption but my blood can wash away the spots thereof? An old proverb there is, and that most true – A living dog is better than a dead lion; oh that it would please her good grace to give me life, yea, the life of a dog, if I might but live and kiss her feet, and spend both life and all in her honourable service."

But Arundel could not save him – would not have saved him, perhaps, had he been able – and he had only to face the end with such resolution as he could command.

The next morning, at nine o'clock, Warwick and Sir John Gates heard mass in the Tower chapel; the two Seymours were again present with Courtenay: and before Gates received the sacrament, he said a few words of regret to the latter for his long imprisonment, of which he admitted himself in part the cause. On leaving the chapel Warwick was taken back to his room, and learned that he was respited. Gates joined Palmer, who was walking with Watson in the garden, and talking with the groups of gentlemen who were collected there. Immediately after, the duke was brought out. "Sir John," he said to Gates, "God have mercy on us; forgive me as I forgive you, although you and your council have brought us hither." "I forgive you, my lord," Gates answered, "as I would be forgiven; yet it was you and your authority that was the only original cause of all." They bowed each. The duke passed on, and the procession moved forward to Tower Hill.

The last words of a worthless man are in themselves of little moment; but the effect of the dying speech of Northumberland lends to it an artificial importance. Whether to the latest moment he hoped for his life, or whether, divided between atheism and superstition, he thought, if any religion was true, Romanism was true, and it was prudent not to throw away a chance, who can tell? At all events, he mounted the scaffold with Heath, the Bishop of Worcester, at his side; and then deliberately said to the crowd, that his rebellion and his present fall were owing to the false preachers who had led him to err from the Catholic faith of Christ; the fathers and the saints had ever agreed in one doctrine; the present generation were the first that had dared to follow their private opinions; and in England and in Germany, where error had taken deepest root, there had followed war, famine, rebellion, misery, tokens all of them of God's displeasure. Therefore, as they loved their country, as they valued their souls, he implored his hearers to turn, all of them, and turn at once, to the church which they had left; in which church he, from the bottom of his heart, avowed his own steadfast belief. For himself he called them all to witness that he died in the one true Catholic faith; to which, if he had been brought sooner, he would not have been in his present calamity.

He then knelt; "I beseech you all," he said again, "to believe that I die in the Catholic faith." He repeated the *Miserere* psalm, the psalm *De Profundis*, and the *Paternoster*. The executioner, as usual, begged his pardon. "I have deserved a thousand deaths," he muttered. He made the sign of the cross upon the saw-dust, and kissed it, then laid down his head, and perished.

The shame of the apostasy shook down the frail edifice of the Protestant constitution, to be raised again in suffering, as the first foundations of it had been laid, by purer hands and nobler spirits. In his better years Northumberland had been a faithful subject and a fearless soldier, and, with a master's hand over him, he might have lived with integrity, and died with honour. Opportunity tempted his ambition – ambition betrayed him into crime – and, given over to his lower nature, he climbed to the highest round of the political ladder, to fall and perish like a craven. He was one of those many men who can follow worthily, yet cannot lead; and the virtue of the beginning was not less real than the ignominy of the end.

## THE SPANISH MARRIAGE

The trials of the last six months had begun to tell upon Mary's understanding: she was ill with hysterical longings; ill with the passions which Gardiner had kindled and Paget disappointed. A lady who slept in her room told Noailles that she could speak to no one without impatience, and that she believed the whole world was in league to keep her husband from her. She found fault with every one – even with the prince himself. Why had he not written? she asked again and again. Why had she never received one courteous word from him? If she heard of merchants or sailors arriving from Spain, she would send for them and question them; and some would tell her that the prince was said to have little heart for his business in England; others terrified her with tales of fearful fights upon the seas; and others brought her news of the French squadrons that were on the watch in the Channel. She would start out of her sleep at night, picturing a thousand terrors, and among them one to which all else were insignificant, that her prince, who had taken such wild possession of her imagination, had no answering feeling for herself – that, with her growing years and wasted figure, she could never win him to love her.

"The unfortunate queen," wrote Henry of France, "will learn the truth at last. She will wake too late, in misery and remorse, to know that she has filled the realm with blood for an object which, when she has gained it, will bring nothing but affliction to herself or to her people."

But the darkest season has its days of sunshine, and Mary's trials were for the present over. If the statesmen were disloyal, the clergy and the Universities appreciated her services to the church, and, in the midst of her trouble, Oxford congratulated her on having been raised up for the restoration of life and light to England. More pleasant than this pleasant flattery was the arrival, on the 19th of June, of the Marquis delas Navas from Spain, with the news that by that time the prince was on his way.

It was even so. Philip had submitted to his unwelcome destiny, and six thousand troops being required pressingly by the emperor in the Low Countries, they attended him for his escort. A paper of advices was drawn for the prince's use by Renard, directing him how to accommodate himself to his barbarous fortune. Neither soldiers nor mariners would be allowed to land. The noblemen, therefore, who formed his retinue, were advised to bring Spanish musketeers, disguised in liveries, in the place of pages and lacqueys; their arms could be concealed amidst the baggage. The war would be an excuse for the noblemen being armed themselves, and the prince, on landing, should have a shirt of mail under his doublet. As to manner, he must endeavour to be affable: he would have to hunt with the young lords, and to make presents to them; and, with whatever difficulty, he must learn a few words of English, to exchange the ordinary salutations. As a friend, Renard recommended Paget to him; he would find Paget "a man of sense."

Philip, who was never remarkable for personal courage, may be pardoned for having come reluctantly to a country where he had to bring men-at-arms for servants, and his own cook for fear of being poisoned. The sea, too, was hateful to him, for he suffered miserably from sickness. Nevertheless, he was coming, and with him such a retinue of gallant gentlemen as the world has rarely seen together. The Marquis de los Valles, Gonzaga, d'Aguilar, Medina Celi, Antonio de Toledo, Diego de Mendoza, the Count de Feria, the Duke of Alva, Count Egmont, and Count Horn – men whose stories are written in the annals of two worlds: some in letters of glorious light, some in letters of blood which shall never be washed out while the history of mankind survives. Whether for evil or good, they were not the meek innocents for whom Renard had at one time asked so anxiously.

In company with these noblemen was Sir Thomas Gresham, charged with half a million of money in bullion, out of the late arrivals from the New World; which the emperor, after taking security from the London merchants, had lent the queen, perhaps to enable her to make her marriage palatable by the restoration of the currency.

Thus preciously freighted, the Spanish fleet, a hundred and fifty ships, large and small, sailed from Corunna at the beginning of July. The voyage was weary and wretched. The sea-sickness prostrated both the prince and the troops, and to the sea-sickness was added the terror of the French – a terror, as it happened, needless, for the English exiles, by whom the prince was to have been intercepted, had, in the last few weeks, melted away from the French service, with the exception of a few who were at Scilly. Sir Peter Carew, for some unknown reason, had written to ask for his pardon, and had gone to Italy; but the change was recent and unknown, and the ships stole along in silence, the orders of the prince being that not a salute should be fired to catch the ear of an enemy. At last, on the 19th of July, the white cliffs of Freshwater were sighted; Lord Howard lay at the Needles with the English fleet; and on Friday, the 20th, at three o'clock in the afternoon, the flotilla was safely anchored in Southampton Water.

The queen was on her way to Winchester, where she arrived the next morning, and either in attendance upon her, or waiting at Southampton, was almost the entire peerage of England. Having made up their minds to endure the marriage, the lords resolved to give Philip the welcome which was due to the husband of their sovereign, and in the uncertain temper of the people, their presence might be necessary to protect his person from insult or from injury.

It was an age of glitter, pomp, and pageantry; the anchors were no sooner down, than a barge was in readiness, with twenty rowers in the queen's colours of green and white; and Arundel, Pembroke, Shrewsbury, Derby, and other lords went off to the vessel which carried the royal standard of Castile. Philip's natural manner was cold and stiff, but he had been schooled into graciousness. Exhausted by his voyage, he accepted delightedly the instant invitation to go on shore, and he entered the barge accompanied by the Duke of Alva. A crowd of gentlemen was waiting to receive him at the landing-place. As he stepped out – not perhaps without some natural nervousness and sharp glances round him – the whole assemblage knelt. A salute was fired from the batteries, and Lord Shrewsbury presented him with the order of the Garter. An enthusiastic eye-witness thus describes Philip's appearance:

"Of visage he is well favoured, with a broad forehead and grey eyes, straight-nosed and manly countenance. From the forehead to the point of his chin his face groweth small. His pace is princely, and gait so straight and upright as he loseth no inch of his height; with a yellow head and a yellow beard; and thus to conclude, he is so well proportioned of body, arm, leg, and every other limb to the same, as nature cannot work a more perfect pattern, and, as I have learned, of the age of 28 years. His majesty I judge to be of a stout stomach, pregnant-witted, and of most gentle nature."

Sir Anthony Brown approached, leading a horse with a saddlecloth of crimson velvet, embroidered with gold and pearls. He presented the steed, with a Latin speech, signifying that he was his highness's Master of the Horse; and Philip, mounting, went direct to Southampton church, the English and Spanish noblemen attending bareheaded, to offer thanks for his safe arrival. From the church he was conducted to a house which had been furnished from the royal stores for his reception. Everything was, of course, magnificent. Only there had been one single oversight. Wrought upon the damask hangings, in conspicuous letters, were observed the ominous words, "Henry, by the Grace of God, King of England, France, and Ireland, and Supreme Head of the Church of England."

Here the prince was to remain till Monday to recover from his voyage; perhaps to ascertain, before he left the neighbourhood of his own fleet, the humour of the barbarians among whom he had arrived. In Latin (he was unable to speak French) he addressed the lords on the causes which had brought him to England, the chief among those causes being the manifest will of God, to which he felt himself bound to submit. It was noticed that he never lifted his cap in speaking to any one, but he evidently endeavoured to be courteous. With a stomach unrecovered from the sea, and disdaining precautions, he sate down on the night of his arrival to a public English supper; he even drained a tankard of ale, as an example, he said, to his Spanish companions. The first evening passed off well, and he retired to seek such rest as the strange land and strange people, the altered diet, and the firing of guns, which never ceased through the summer night, would allow him.

Another feature of his new country awaited Philip in the morning (July 21); he had come from the sunny plains of Castile; from his window at Southampton he looked out upon a steady downfall of July rain. Through the cruel torrent he made his way to the church again to mass, and afterwards Gardiner came to him from the queen. In the afternoon the sky cleared, and the Duchess of Alva, who had accompanied her husband, was taken out in a barge upon Southampton Water. Both English and Spaniards exerted themselves to be mutually pleasing; but the situation was not of a kind which it was desirable to protract. Six thousand Spanish troops were cooped in the close uneasy transports, forbidden to land lest they should provoke the jealousy of the people; and when, on Sunday (July 22), his highness had to undergo a public dinner, in which English servants only were allowed to attend upon him, the Castilian lords, many of whom believed that they had come to England on a bootless errand, broke out into murmurs.

Monday came at last; the rain fell again, and the wind howled. The baggage was sent forward in the morning in the midst of the tempest. Philip lingered in hopes of a change; but no change came, and after an early dinner the trumpet sounded to horse. Lords, knights, and gentlemen had thronged into the town, from curiosity or interest, out of all the counties round. Before the prince mounted it was reckoned, with uneasiness, that as many as four thousand cavaliers, under no command, were collected to join the procession.

A grey gelding was led up for Philip; he wrapped himself in a scarlet cloak, and started to meet his bride – to complete a sacrifice the least congenial, perhaps, which ever policy of state extracted from a prince.

The train could move but slowly. Two miles beyond the gates a drenched rider, spattered with chalk mud, was seen galloping towards them; on reaching the prince he presented him with a ring from the queen, and begged his highness, in her majesty's name, to come no further. The messenger could not explain the cause, being unable to speak any language which Philip could understand, and visions of commotion instantly presented themselves, mixed, it may be, with a hope that the bitter duty might yet be escaped. Alva was immediately at his master's side; they reined up, and were asking each other anxiously what should next be done, when an English lord exclaimed in French, with courteous irony, "Our queen, sire, loves your highness so tenderly that she would not have you come to her in such wretched weather." The hope, if hope there had been, died in its birth; before sunset, with drenched garments and draggled plume, the object of so many anxieties arrived within the walls of Winchester.

To the cathedral he went first, wet as he was. Whatever Philip of Spain was entering upon, whether it was a marriage or a massacre, a state intrigue or a midnight murder, his opening step was ever to seek a blessing from the holy wafer. He entered, kissed the crucifix, and knelt and prayed before the altar; then taking his seat in the choir, he remained while the choristers sang a *Te Deum laudamus*, till the long aisles grew dim in the summer twilight, and he was conducted by torch-light to the Deanery.

The queen was at the bishop's palace, but a few hundred yards distant. Philip, doubtless, could have endured the postponement of an interview till morning; but Mary could not wait, and the same night he was conducted into the presence of his haggard bride, who now, after a life of misery, believed herself at the open gate of Paradise. Let the curtain fall over the meeting, let it close also over the wedding solemnities which followed with due splendour two days later. There are scenes in life which we regard with pity too deep for words. The unhappy queen, unloved, unlovable, yet with her parched heart thirsting for affection, was flinging herself upon a breast to which an iceberg was warm; upon a man to whom love was an unmeaning word, except as the most brutal of passions. For a few months she created for herself an atmosphere of unreality. She saw in Philip the ideal of her imagination, and in Philip's feelings the reflex of her own; but the dream passed away – her love for her husband remained; but remained only to be a torture to her. With a broken spirit and bewildered understanding, she turned to Heaven for comfort, and, instead of heaven, she saw only the false roof of her creed painted to imitate and shut out the sky.

## THE RECONCILIATION OF THE KINGDOM

And now St. Andrew's Day was come; a day, as was then hoped, which would be remembered with awe and gratitude through all ages of English history. Being the festival of the institution of the Order of the Golden Fleece, high mass was sung in the morning in Westminster Abbey; Philip, Alva, and Ruy Gomez attended in their robes, with six hundred Spanish cavaliers. The Knights of the Garter were present in gorgeous costume, and nave and transept were thronged with the blended chivalry of England and Castile. It was two o'clock before the service was concluded. Philip returned to the palace to dinner, and the brief November afternoon was drawing in when the parliament reassembled at the palace. At the upper end of the great hall a square platform had now been raised several steps above the floor, on which three chairs were placed as before; two under a canopy of cloth of gold, for the king and queen; a third on the right, removed a little distance from them, for the legate. Below the platform, benches were placed longitudinally towards either wall. The bishops sat on the side of the legate, the lay peers opposite them on the left. The Commons sat on rows of cross benches in front, and beyond them were the miscellaneous crowd of spectators, sitting or standing as they could find room. The cardinal, who had passed the morning at Lambeth, was conducted across the water in a state barge by Lord Arundel and six other peers. The king received him at the gate, and, leaving his suite in the care of the Duke of Alva, who was instructed to find them places, he accompanied Philip into the room adjoining the hall, where Mary, whose situation was supposed to prevent her from unnecessary exertion, was waiting for them. The royal procession was formed. Arundel and the Lords passed in to their places. The king and queen, with Pole in his legate's robes, ascended the steps of the platform, and took their seats.

When the stir which had been caused by their entrance was over, Gardiner mounted a tribune; and in the now fast-waning light he bowed to the king and queen, and declared the resolution at which the Houses had arrived. Then turning to the Lords and Commons, he asked if they continued in the same mind. Four hundred voices answered, "We do." "Will you then," he said, "that I proceed in your names to supplicate for our absolution, that we may be received again into the body of the Holy Catholic Church, under the pope, the supreme head thereof?" Again the voices assented. The chancellor drew a scroll from under his robe, ascended the platform, and presented it unfolded on his knee to the queen. The queen looked through it, gave it to Philip, who looked through it also, and returned it. The chancellor then rose and read aloud as follows:

"We, the Lords Spiritual and Temporal, and the Commons of the present parliament assembled, representing the whole body of the realm of England, and dominions of the same, in our own names particularly, and also of the said body universally, in this our supplication directed to your majesties – with most humble suit that it may by your gracious intercession and means be exhibited to the Most Reverend Father in God the Lord Cardinal Pole, Legate, sent specially hither from our Most Holy Father Pope Julius the Third and the See Apostolic of Rome – do declare ourselves very sorry and repentant for the schism and disobedience committed in this realm and dominions of the same, against the said See Apostolic, either by making, agreeing, or executing any laws, ordinances, or commandments against the supremacy of the said See, or otherwise doing or speaking what might impugn the same; offering ourselves, and promising by this our supplication that, for a token and knowledge of our said repentance, we be, and shall be always, ready, under and with the authority of your majesties, to do that which shall be in us for the abrogation and repealing of the said laws and ordinances in this present parliament, as well for ourselves as for the whole body whom we represent. Whereupon we most humbly beseech your majesties, as persons undefiled in the offences of this body towards the Holy See – which nevertheless God by his providence hath made subject to your majesties – so to set forth this, our most humble suit, that we may obtain from the See Apostolic, by the said Most Reverend Father, as well particularly as universally, absolution, release, and discharge from all danger of such censures and sentences as by the laws of the church we be fallen in; and that we may, as children repentant, be received into the bosom and unity of Christ's Church; so as this noble realm, with all the members thereof, may, in unity and perfect obedience to the See Apostolic and pope for the time being, serve God and your majesties, to the furtherance and advancement of his honour and glory."

Having completed the reading, the chancellor again presented the petition. The king and queen went through the forms of intercession, and a secretary read aloud, first, the legate's original commission, and, next, the all-important extended form of it.

Pole's share of the ceremony was now to begin.

He first spoke a few words from his seat: "Much indeed," he said, "the English nation had to thank the Almighty for recalling them to his fold. Once again God had given a token of his special favour to the realm; for as this nation, in the time of the Primitive Church, was the first to be called out of the darkness of heathenism, so now they were the first to whom God had given grace to repent of their schism; and if their repentance was sincere, how would the angels, who rejoice at the conversion of a single sinner, triumph at the recovery of a great and noble people."

He moved to rise; Mary and Philip, seeing that the crisis was approaching, fell on their knees, and the assembly dropped at their example; while, in dead silence, across the dimly-lighted hall, came the low, awful words of the absolution.

"Our Lord Jesus Christ, which with his most precious blood hath redeemed and washed us from all our sins and iniquities, that he might purchase unto himself a glorious spouse without spot or wrinkle, whom the Father hath appointed head over all his Church – he by his mercy absolves you, and we, by apostolic authority given unto us by the Most Holy Lord Pope Julius the Third, his vicegerent on earth, do absolve and deliver you, and every of you, with this whole realm and the dominions thereof, from all heresy and schism, and from all and every judgment, censure, and pain for that cause incurred; and we do restore you again into the unity of our Mother the Holy Church, in the name of the Father, of the Son, and of the Holy Ghost."

Amidst the hushed breathing every tone was audible, and at the pauses were heard the smothered sobs of the queen. "Amen, amen," rose in answer from many voices. Some were really affected; some were caught for the moment with a contagion which it was hard to resist; some threw themselves weeping in each other's arms. King, queen, and parliament, rising from their knees, went immediately – the legate leading – into the chapel of the palace, where the choir, with the rolling organ, sang *Te Deum*; and Pole closed the scene with a benediction from the altar.

"Blessed day for England," cries the Italian describer, in a rapture of devotion. "The people exclaim in ecstasies, we are reconciled to God, we are brought back to God: the king beholds his realm, so lately torn by divisions, at the mercy of the first enemy who would seize upon it, secured on a foundation which never can be shaken: and who can express the joy – who can tell the exultation of the queen? She has shown herself the handmaid of the Lord, and all generations shall call her blessed: she has given her kingdom to God as a thank-offering for those great mercies which He has bestowed upon her."

And the legate; but the legate has described his emotions in his own inimitable manner. Pole went back to Lambeth, not to rest, but to pour out his soul to the Holy Father.

In his last letter he said "he had told his holiness that he had hoped that England would be recovered to the fold at last; yet he had then some fears remaining, so far estranged were the minds of the people from the Holy See, lest at the last moment some compromise might ruin all."

But the godly forwardness of the king and queen had overcome every difficulty; and on that evening, the day of St. Andrew – of Andrew who first brought his brother Peter to Christ – the realm of England had been brought back to its obedience to Peter's See, and through Peter to Christ. The great act had been accomplished, accomplished by the virtue and the labour of the inestimable sovereigns with whom God had blessed the world.

"And oh," he said, "how many things, how great things, may the church our mother, the bride of Christ, promise herself from these her children? Oh piety! oh antient faith! Whoever looks on them will repeat the words of the prophet of the church's early offspring; 'This is the seed which the Lord hath blessed.' How earnestly, how lovingly, did your holiness favour their marriage; a marriage formed after the very pattern of that of our Most High King, who, being Heir of the world, was sent down by his Father from his royal throne, to be at once the Spouse and the Son of the Virgin Mary, and be made the Comforter and the Saviour of mankind: and, in like manner, the greatest of all the princes upon earth, the heir of his father's kingdom, departed from his own broad and happy realms, that he might come hither into this land of trouble, he, too, to be spouse and son of this virgin; for, indeed, though spouse he be, he so bears himself towards her as if he were her son, to aid in the reconciliation of this people to Christ and the church.

"When your holiness first chose me as your legate, the queen was rising up as a rod of incense out of trees of myrrh, and as frankincense out of the desert. And how does she now shine out in loveliness? What a savour does she give forth unto her people. Yea, even as the prophet saith of the mother of Christ, 'before she was in labour she brought forth, before she was delivered she hath borne a man-child.' Who ever yet hath seen it, who has heard of the similitude of it? Shall the earth bring forth in a day, or shall a nation of men be born together? but Mary has brought forth the nation of England before the time of that delivery for which we all are hoping!"

Unable to exhaust itself in words, the Catholic enthusiasm flowed over in processions, in sermons, masses, and *Te Deums*. Gardiner at Paul's Cross, on the Sunday succeeding, confessed his sins in having borne a part in bringing about the schism. Pole rode through the city between the king and queen, with his legate's cross before him, blessing the people. When the news reached Rome Julius first embraced the messenger, then flung himself on his knees, and said a Paternoster. The guns at St. Angelo roared in triumph. There were jubilees and masses of the Holy Ghost, and bonfires, and illuminations, and pardons, and indulgences. In the exuberance of his hopes, the pope sent a nuncio to urge that, in the presence of this great mercy, peace should be made with France, where the king was devoted to the church; the Catholic powers would then have the command of Europe, and the heretics could be destroyed. One thing only seemed forgotten, that the transaction was a bargain. The papal pardon had been thrust upon criminals, whose hearts were so culpably indifferent that it was necessary to bribe them to accept it; and the conditions of the compromise, even yet, were far from concluded.

## THE PERSECUTION BEGINS

From the beginning of the Reformation in 1529, two distinct movements had gone on side by side – the alteration of doctrines, and the emancipation of the laity from papal and ecclesiastical domination. With the first, the contemporaries of Henry VIII., the country gentlemen and the peers, who were the heads of families at the period of Mary's accession, had never sympathised; and the tyranny of the Protestants while they were in power had converted a disapproval which time would have overcome, into active and determined indignation. The papacy was a mixed question; the Pilgrims of Grace in 1536, and the Cornish rebels in 1549, had demanded the restoration of the spiritual primacy to the See of St. Peter, and Henry himself, until Pole and Paul III. called on Europe to unite in a crusade against him, had not determined wholly against some degree of concession. In the pope, as a sovereign who claimed reverence and tribute, who interfered with the laws of the land, and maintained at Rome a supreme court of appeal – who pretended a right to depose kings and absolve subjects from their allegiance – who held a weapon in excommunication as terrible to the laity as Premunire was terrible to ecclesiastics – in the pope under this aspect, only a few insignificant fanatics entertained any kind of interest.

But experience had proved that to a nation cut off from the centre of Catholic union, the maintenance of orthodoxy was impossible: the supremacy of the pope, therefore, came back as a tolerated feature in the return to the Catholic faith, and the ecclesiastical courts were reinstated in authority to check unlicensed extravagance of opinion. Their restored power, however, was over opinion only; wherever the pretensions of the church would come in collision with the political constitution, wherever they menaced the independence of the temporal magistrate or the tenure of property, there the progress of restoration was checked by the rock, and could eat no further into the soil. The pope and the clergy recovered their titular rank, and in one direction unhappily they recovered the reality of power. But the temporal spoils of the struggle remained with the laity, and if the clergy lifted a hand to retake them, their weapons would be instantly wrenched from their grasp.

If the genuine friends of human freedom had acquiesced without resistance in this conclusion, if the nobility had contented themselves with securing their worldly and political interests, and had made no effort to restrain or modify the exercise of the authority which they were giving back, they might be accused of having accepted a dishonourable compromise. But they did what they could. They worked with such legal means as were in their power, and for two parliaments they succeeded in keeping persecution at bay; they failed in the third, but failed only after a struggle. The Protestants themselves had created, by their own misconduct, the difficulty of defending them; and armed unconstitutional resistance was an expedient to be resorted to, only when it had been seen how the clergy would conduct themselves. English statesmen may be pardoned if they did not anticipate the passions to which the guardians of orthodoxy were about to abandon themselves. Parliament had maintained the independence of the English courts of law. It had maintained the Premunire. It had forbidden the succession to be tampered with. If this was not everything, it was something – something which in the end would be the undoing of all the rest.

The court and the bishops, however, were for the present absolute in their own province. The persecuting acts were once more upon the Statute Book; and when the realities of the debates in parliament had disappeared, the cardinal and the queen could again give the rein to their imagination. They had called up a phantom out of its grave, and they persuaded themselves that they were witnessing the resurrection of the spirit of truth, that heresy was about to vanish from off the English soil, like an exhalation of the morning, at the brightness of the papal return. The chancellor and the clergy were springing at the leash like hounds with the game in view, fanaticism and revenge lashing them forward. If the temporal schemes of the court were thwarted, it was, perhaps, because Heaven desired that exclusive attention should be given first to the salvation of souls.

For all past political offences, therefore, there was now an amnesty, and such prisoners as remained unexecuted for Wyatt's conspiracy were released from the Tower on the 18th of January. On the 25th a hundred and sixty priests walked in procession through the London streets, chanting litanies, with eight bishops walking after them, and Bonner carrying the host. On the 28th the cardinal issued his first general instructions. The bishops were directed to call together their clergy in every diocese in England, and to inform them of the benevolent love of the Holy Father, and of the arrival of the legate with powers to absolve them from their guilt.

They were to relate the acts of the late parliament, with the reconciliation and absolution of the Lords and Commons; and they were to give general notice that authority had been restored to the ecclesiastical courts, to proceed against the enemies of the faith, and punish them according to law.

A day was then to be fixed on which the clergy should appear with their confessions, and be received into the church. In the assignment of their several penances, a distinction was to be made between those who had taught heresy and those who had merely lapsed into it.

When the clergy had been reconciled, they were again in turn to exhort the laity in all churches and cathedrals, to accept the grace which was offered to them; and that they might understand that they were not at liberty to refuse the invitation, a time was assigned to them within which their submissions must be all completed. A book was to be kept in every diocese, where the names of those who were received were to be entered. A visitation was to be held throughout the country at the end of the spring, and all who had not complied before Easter day, or who, after compliance, "had returned to their vomit", would be proceeded against with the utmost severity of the law.

The introduction of the Register was the Inquisition under another name. There was no limit, except in the humanity or the prudence of the bishops, to the tyranny which they would be enabled to exercise. The cardinal professed to desire that, before heretics were punished with death, mild means should first be tried with them; the meaning which he attached to the words was illustrated in an instant example.

The instructions were the signal for the bishops to commence business. On the day of their appearance, Gardiner, Bonner, Tunstal, and three other prelates, formed a court in

St. Mary Overy's Church, in Southwark; and Hooper, and Rogers, a canon of St. Paul's, were brought up before them.

Rogers had been distinguished in the first bright days of Protestantism. He had been a fellow-labourer with Tyndal and Coverdale, at Antwerp, in the translation of the Bible. Afterwards, taking a German wife, he lived for a time at Wittenberg, not unknown, we may be sure, to Martin Luther. On the accession of Edward, he returned to England, and worked among the London clergy till the end of the reign; and on Mary's accession he was one of the preachers at Paul's Cross who had dared to speak against the reaction. He had been rebuked by the council, and his friends had urged him to fly; but, like Cranmer, he thought that duty required him to stay at his post, and, in due time, without, however, having given fresh provocation, he was shut up in Newgate by Bonner.

Hooper, when the unfortunate garment controversy was brought to an end, had shown by his conduct in his diocese that in one instance at least doctrinal fanaticism was compatible with the loftiest excellence. While the great world was scrambling for the church property, Hooper was found petitioning the council for leave to augment impoverished livings out of his own income. In the hall of his palace at Gloucester a profuse hospitality was offered daily to those who were most in need of it. The poor of the city were invited by relays to solid meat dinners, and the bishop with the courtesy of a gentleman dined with them, and treated them with the same respect as if they had been the highest in the land. He was one of the first persons arrested after Mary's accession, and the cross of persecution at once happily made his peace with Ridley. In an affectionate interchange of letters, the two confessors exhorted each other to constancy in the end which both foresaw, determining "if they could not overthrow, at least, to shake those high altitudes" of spiritual tyranny. The Fleet prison had now been Hooper's house for eighteen months. At first, on payment of heavy fees to the warden, he had lived in some degree of comfort; but as soon as his deprivation was declared, Gardiner ordered that he should be confined in one of the common prisoners' wards; where "with a wicked man and a wicked woman" for his companions, with a bed of straw and a rotten counterpane, the prison sink on one side of his cell and Fleet ditch on the other, he waited till it would please parliament to permit the dignitaries of the Church to murder him.

These were the two persons with whom the Marian persecution opened. On their appearance in the court, they were required briefly to make their submission. They attempted to argue; but they were told that when parliament had determined a thing, private men were not to call it in question, and they were allowed twenty-four hours to make up their minds. As they were leaving the church Hooper was heard to say, "Come, brother Rogers, must we two take this matter first in hand and fry these faggots?" "Yea, sir, with God's grace," Rogers answered. "Doubt not," Hooper said, "but God will give us strength."

They were remanded to prison. The next morning they were brought again before the court. "The queen's mercy" was offered them, if they would recant; they refused, and they were sentenced to die. Rogers asked to be allowed to take leave of his wife and children. Gardiner, with a savage taunt, rejected the request. The day of execution was left uncertain. They were sent to Newgate to wait the queen's pleasure. On the 30th, Taylor of Hadley, Laurence Sandars, rector of All Hallows, and the illustrious Bradford, were passed through the same forms with the same results. Another, a notorious preacher, called Cardmaker, flinched, and made his submission.

Rogers was to "break the ice," as Bradford described it. On the morning of the 4th of February the wife of the keeper of Newgate came to his bedside. He was sleeping soundly, and she woke him with difficulty to let him know that he was wanted. The Bishop of London was waiting, she said, to degrade him from the priesthood, and he was then to go out and die. Rubbing his eyes, and collecting himself, he hurried on his clothes. "If it be thus." he said, "I need not tie my points." Hooper had been sent for also for the ceremony of degradation. The vestments used in the mass were thrown over them, and were then one by one removed. They were pronounced deposed from the priestly office, incapable of offering further sacrifice – except, indeed, the only acceptable sacrifice which man can ever offer, the sacrifice of himself. Again Rogers entreated permission to see his wife, and again he was refused.

The two friends were then parted. Hooper was to suffer at Gloucester, and returned to his cell; Rogers was committed to the sheriff, and led out to Smithfield. The Catholics had affected to sneer at the faith of their rivals. There was a general conviction among them, which was shared probably by Pole and Gardiner, that the Protestants would all flinch at the last; that they had no "doctrine that would abide the fire." When Rogers appeared, therefore, the exultation of the people in his constancy overpowered the horror of his fate, and he was received with rounds of cheers. His family, whom he was forbidden to part with in private, were waiting on the way to see him – his wife with nine little ones at her side and a tenth upon her breast – and they, too, welcomed him with hysterical cries of joy, as if he were on his way to a festival. Sir Robert Rochester was in attendance at the stake to report his behaviour. At the last moment he was offered pardon if he would give way, but in vain. The fire was lighted. The suffering seemed to be nothing. He bathed his hands in the flame as "if it was cold water," raised his eyes to heaven, and died.

The same night a party of the royal guard took charge of Hooper, the order of whose execution was arranged by a mandate from the crown. As "an obstinate, false, and detestable heretic," he was to be burned in the city "which he had infected with his pernicious doctrines;" and "forasmuch as being a vainglorious person, and delighting in his tongue," he "might persuade the people into agreement with him, had he liberty to use it," care was to be taken that he should not speak either at the stake or on his way to it. He was carried down on horseback by easy stages; and on the forenoon of Thursday, the 7th, he dined at Cirencester, "at a woman's house who had always hated the truth, and spoken all evil she could of him." This woman had shared in the opinion that Protestants had no serious convictions, and had often expressed her belief that Hooper, particularly, would fail if brought to the trial. She found that both in him and in his creed there was more than she had supposed; and "perceiving the cause of his coming, she lamented his case with tears, and showed him all the friendship she could."

At five in the evening he arrived at Gloucester. The road, for a mile outside the town, was lined with people, and the mayor was in attendance, with an escort, to prevent a rescue. But the feeling was rather of awe and expectation, and those who loved Hooper best knew that the highest service which he could render to his faith was to die for it.

A day's interval of preparation was allowed him, with a private room. He was in the custody of the sheriff; "and there was this difference observed between the keepers of the bishops' prisons and the keepers of the crown prisons, that the bishops' keepers were ever cruel; the keepers of the crown prisons showed, for the most part, such favour as they might." After a sound night's rest, Hooper rose early, and passed the morning in solitary prayer. In the course of the day, young Sir Anthony Kingston, one of the commissioners appointed to superintend the execution, expressed a wish to see him. Kingston was an old acquaintance, Hooper having been the means of bringing him out of evil ways. He entered the room unannounced. Hooper was on his knees, and, looking round at the intruder, did not at first know him. Kingston told him his name, and then, bursting into tears, said:

"Oh, consider; life is sweet and death is bitter; therefore, seeing life may be had, desire to live, for life hereafter may do good."

Hooper answered:

"I thank you for your counsel, yet it is not so friendly as I could have wished it to be. True it is, alas! Master Kingston, that death is bitter and life is sweet; therefore I have settled myself, through the strength of God's Holy Spirit, patiently to pass through the fire prepared for me, desiring you and others to commend me to God's mercy in your prayers."

"Well, my Lord," said Kingston, "then there is no remedy, and I will take my leave. I thank God that ever I knew you, for God appointed you to call me, being a lost child. I was both an adulterer and a fornicator, and God, by your good instruction, brought me to the forsaking of the same."

They parted, the tears on both their faces. Other friends were admitted afterwards. The queen's orders were little thought of, for Hooper had won the hearts of the guard on his way from London. In the evening the mayor and aldermen came, with the sheriffs, to shake hands with him. "It was a sign of their good will," he said, "and a proof that they had not forgotten the lessons which he used to teach them." He begged the sheriffs that there might be "a quick fire, to make an end shortly;" and for himself he would be as obedient as they could wish.

"If you think I do amiss in anything," he said, "hold up your fingers, and I have done; for I am not come hither as one enforced or compelled to die; I might have had my life, as is well known, with worldly gain, if I would have accounted my doctrine falsehood and heresy."

In the evening, at his own request, he was left alone. He slept undisturbed the early part of the night. From the time that he awoke till the guard entered, he was on his knees.

The morning was windy and wet. The scene of the execution was an open space opposite the college, near a large elm tree, where Hooper had been accustomed to preach. Several thousand people were collected to see him suffer; some had climbed the tree, and were seated in the storm and rain among the leafless branches. A company of priests were in a room over the college gates, looking out with pity or satisfaction, as God or the devil was in their hearts.

"Alas!" said Hooper, when he was brought out, "why be all these people assembled here, and speech is prohibited me?" He had suffered in prison from sciatica, and was lame, but he limped cheerfully along with a stick, and smiled when he saw the stake. At the foot of it he knelt; and as he began to pray, a box was brought, and placed on a stool before his eyes, which he was told contained his pardon if he would recant.

"Away with it;" Hooper only cried; "away with it!"

"Despatch him, then," Lord Chandos said, "seeing there is no remedy."

He was undressed to his shirt, in the cold; a pound of gunpowder was tied between his legs, and as much more under either arm; he was fastened with an iron hoop to the stake, and he assisted with his own hands to arrange the faggots round him.

The fire was then brought, but the wood was green; the dry straw only kindled, and burning for a few moments was blown away by the wind. A violent flame paralysed the nerves at once, a slow one was torture. More faggots were thrown in, and again lighted, and this time the martyr's face was singed and scorched; but again the flames sank, and the hot damp sticks smouldered round his legs. He wiped his eyes with his hands, and cried, "For God's love, good people, let me have more fire!" A third supply of dry fuel was laid about him, and this time the powder exploded, but it had been ill placed, or was not enough. "Lord Jesu, have mercy on me!" he exclaimed; "Lord Jesu, receive my spirit!" These were his last articulate words; but his lips were long seen to move, and he continued to beat his breast with his hands. It was not till after three-quarters of an hour of torment that he at last expired.

The same day, at the same hour, Rowland Taylor was burnt on Aldham Common, in Suffolk. Laurance Sandars had been destroyed the day before at Coventry, kissing the stake, and crying, "Welcome the cross of Christ! welcome everlasting life!" The first-fruits of the Whitehall pageant were gathered. By the side of the rhetoric of the hysterical dreamer who presided in that vain melodrama, let me place a few words addressed by the murdered Bishop of

Gloucester to his friends, a week before his sentence.

"The grace of God be with you, amen. I did write unto you of late, and told you what extremity the parliament had concluded upon concerning religion, suppressing the truth, and setting forth the untruth; intending to cause all men, by extremity, to forswear themselves; and to take again for the head of the church him that is neither head nor member of it, but a very enemy, as the word of God and all ancient writers do record. And for lack of law and authority they will use force and extremity, which have been the arguments to defend the pope and popery since their authority first began in the world. But now is the time of trial, to see whether we fear more God or man. It was an easy thing to hold with Christ whilst the prince and the world held with him; but now the world hateth him, it is the true trial who be his.

"Wherefore in the name, and in the virtue, strength, and power of his Holy Spirit, prepare yourselves in any case to adversity and constancy. Let us not run away when it is most time to fight. Remember, none shall be crowned but such as fight manfully; and he that endureth to the end shall be saved. Ye must now turn your cogitations from the perils you see, and mark the felicity that followeth the peril – either victory in this world of your enemies, or else a surrender of this life to inherit the everlasting kingdom. Beware of beholding too much the felicity or misery of this world; for the consideration and too earnest love or fear of either of them draweth from God. Wherefore think with yourselves as touching the felicity of the world, it is good; but none otherwise than it standeth with the favour of God; it is to be kept, but yet so far forth as by keeping it we lose not God. It is good abiding and tarrying still among our friends here, but yet so that we tarry not therewithal in God's displeasure, and hereafter dwell with the devils in fire everlasting. There is nothing under God but may be kept, so that God, being above all things we have, be not lost. Of adversity judge the same. Imprisonment is painful, but yet liberty upon evil conditions is more painful. The prisons stink; but yet not so much as sweet houses, where the fear and true honour of God lack. I must be alone and solitary; it is better so to be, and have God with me, than to be in company with the wicked. Loss of goods is great, but loss of God's grace and favour is greater. I am a poor simple creature, and cannot tell how to answer before such a great sort of noble, learned, and wise men. It is better to make answer before the pomp and pride of wicked men, than to stand naked, in the sight of all heaven and earth, before the just God at the latter day. I shall die by the hands of the cruel men; but he is blessed that loseth this life full of miseries, and findeth the life of eternal joys. It is pain and grief to depart from goods and friends; but yet not so much as to depart from grace and heaven itself. Wherefore there is neither felicity nor adversity of this world that can appear to be great, if it be weighed with the joys or pains in the world to come."

Of five who had been sentenced, four were thus despatched. Bradford, the fifth, was respited, in the hope that the example might tell upon him. Six more were waiting their condemnation in Bonner's prisons. The enemies of the church were to submit or die. So said Gardiner, in the name of the English priesthood, with the passion of a fierce revenge. So said the legate and the queen, in the delirious belief that they were chosen instruments of Providence.

So, however, did not say the English lay statesmen. The first and unexpected effect was to produce a difference of opinion in the court itself. Philip, to whom Renard had insisted on the necessity of more moderate measures, found it necessary to clear himself of responsibility; and the day after Hooper suffered, Alphonso a Castro, the king's chaplain, preached a sermon in the royal presence, in which he denounced the execution, and inveighed against the tyranny of the bishops. The Lords of the Council "talked strangely;" and so deep was the indignation, that the Flemish ambassador again expected Gardiner's destruction. Paget refused to act with him in the council any more, and Philip himself talked more and more of going abroad. Renard, from the tone of his correspondence, believed evidently at this moment that the game of the church was played out and lost. He wrote to the emperor to entreat that when the king went he might not himself be left behind; he was held responsible by the people for the queen's misdoings; and a party of the young nobility had sworn to kill him.

Among the people the constancy of the martyrs had called out a burst of admiration. It was rumoured that bystanders had endeavoured to throw themselves into the fire to die at their side. A prisoner, on examination before Bonner, was asked if he thought he could bear the flame. You may try me, if you will, he said. A candle was brought, and he held his hand, without flinching, in the blaze. With such a humour abroad, it seemed to Renard that the Lords had only to give the signal, and the queen and the bishops would be overwhelmed.

He expected the movement in the spring. It is singular that, precisely as in the preceding winter, the deliberate intentions of moderate and competent persons were anticipated and defeated by a partial and premature conspiracy. At the end of February a confederate revealed a project for an insurrection, partly religious and partly agrarian. Placards were to be issued simultaneously in all parts of the country, declaring that the queen's pregnancy was a delusion, and that she intended to pass upon the nation a supposititious child; the people were, therefore, invited to rise in arms, drive out the Spaniards, revolutionise religion, tear down the enclosures of the commons, and proclaim Courtenay king under the title of Edward VII. In such a scheme the lords and country gentlemen could bear no part. They could not risk a repetition of the popular rebellions of the late reign, and they resolved to wait the issue of the queen's pregnancy, while they watched over the safety of Elizabeth. The project of the court was now to send her to Flanders, where she was to remain under charge of the emperor; if possible, she was to be persuaded to go thither of her own accord; if she could not be persuaded, she would be otherwise removed. Lord William Howard, her constant guardian, requested permission to see and speak with her, and learn her own feelings. He was refused; but he went to her notwithstanding, and had a long private interview with her; and the court could only talk bitterly of his treason among themselves, make propositions to send him to the Tower which they durst not execute, and devise some other method of dealing with their difficulty.

## THE UNHAPPY QUEEN

For thirty-five years the two great Catholic powers had been wrestling with but brief interruption. The advantage to either had been as trifling as the causes of their quarrel were insignificant. Their revenues were anticipated, their credit was exhausted, yet year after year languid armies struggled into collision. Across the Alps in Italy, and along the frontiers of Burgundy and the Low Countries, towns and villages, and homesteads were annually sacked, and peasants and their families destroyed – for what it were vain to ask, except it was for some poor shadow of imagined honour. Two mighty princes believed themselves justified in the sight of Heaven in squandering their subjects' treasure and their subjects' blood, because the pride of each forbade him to be the first in volunteering insignificant concessions. France had conquered Savoy and part of Piedmont, and had pushed forward its northern frontier to Marienbourg and Metz: the emperor held Lombardy, Parma, and Naples, and Navarre was annexed to Spain. The quarrel might have easily been ended by mutual restitution; yet the Peace of Cambray, the Treaty of Nice, and the Peace of Crêpy, lasted only while the combatants were taking breath; and those who would attribute the extravagances of human folly to supernatural influence might imagine that the great discord between the orthodox powers had been permitted to give time for the Reformation to strike its roots into the soil of Europe. But a war which could be carried on only by loans at sixteen per cent. was necessarily near its conclusion. The apparent recovery of England to the church revived hopes which the Peace of Passau and the dissolution of the Council of Trent had almost extinguished; and, could a reconciliation be effected at last, and could Philip obtain the disposal of the military strength of England in the interests of the papacy, it might not even yet be too late to lay the yoke of orthodoxy on the Germans, and, in a Catholic interpretation of the Parable of the Supper, "compel them to come in."

Mary, who had heard herself compared to the Virgin, and Pole, who imagined the Prince of Spain to be the counterpart of the Redeemer of mankind, indulged their fancy in large expectations. Philip was the Solomon who was to raise up the temple of the Lord, which the emperor, who was a man of war, had not been allowed to build: and France, at the same time, was not unwilling to listen to proposals. The birth of Mary's child was expected in a few weeks, when England would, as a matter of course, become more decisively Imperialist, and Henry, whose invasion of the Netherlands had failed in the previous summer, was ready now to close the struggle while it could be ended on equal and honourable terms.

A conference was, therefore, agreed upon, in which England was to mediate. A village in the Calais Pale was selected as the place of assembly, and Pole, Gardiner, Paget, and Pembroke were chosen to arrange the terms of a general peace, with the Bishop of Arras, the Cardinal of Lorraine, and Montmorency. The time pitched upon was that at which, so near as the queen could judge, she would herself bring into the world the offspring which was to be the hope of England and mankind; and the great event should, if possible, precede the first meeting of the plenipotentiaries.

The queen herself commenced her preparations with infinite earnestness, and, as a preliminary votive offering, she resolved to give back to the church such of the abbey property as remained in the hands of the crown. Her debts were now as high as ever. The Flanders correspondence was repeating the heavy story of loans and bills. Promises to pay were falling due, and there were no resources to meet them, and the Israelite leeches were again fastened on the commonwealth. Nevertheless, the sacrifice should be made; the more difficult it was, the more favourably it would be received; and, on the 28th of March, she sent for the Lord Treasurer, and announced her intention. "If he told her that her estate would not bear it, she must reply," she said, "that

she valued the salvation of her soul beyond all earthly things."
As soon as parliament could meet and give its sanction, she
would restore the first-fruits also to the Holy See. She must
work for God as God had worked for her.

About the 20th of April she withdrew to Hampton
Court for entire quiet. The rockers and the nurses were
in readiness, and a cradle stood open to receive the royal
infant. Priests and bishops sang Litanies through the London
streets; a procession of ecclesiastics in cloth of gold and tissue
marched round Hampton Court Palace, headed by Philip in
person; Gardiner walked at his side, while Mary gazed from
a window. Not only was the child assuredly coming, but its
sex was decided on, and circulars were drawn and signed
both by the king and queen, with blanks only for the month
and day, announcing to ministers of state, to ambassadors,
and to foreign sovereigns, the birth of a prince.

On the 30th, the happy moment was supposed to have
arrived; a message was sent off to London, announcing the
commencement of the pains. The bells were set ringing in all
the churches; *Te Deum* was sung in St. Paul's; priests wrote
sermons; bonfires were piled ready for lighting, and tables
were laid out in the streets. The news crossed the Channel
to Antwerp, and had grown in the transit. The great bell of
the cathedral was rung for the actual birth. The vessels in
the river fired salutes. "The regent sent the English mariners
a hundred crowns to drink," and, "they made themselves in
readiness to show some worthy triumph upon the waters."

But the pains passed off without result; and whispers
began to be heard, that there was, perhaps, a mistake of a
more considerable kind. Mary, however, had herself no sort
of misgiving. She assured her attendants that all was well,
and that she felt the motion of her child. The physicians

professed to be satisfied, and the priests were kept at work at the Litanies. Up and down the streets they marched, through city and suburb, park and square; torches flared along Cheapside at midnight behind the Holy Sacrament, and five hundred poor men and women from the almshouses walked two and two, telling their beads in their withered fingers: then all the boys of all the schools were set in motion, and the ushers and the masters came after them; clerks, canons, bishops, mayor, aldermen, officers of guilds. Such marching, such chanting, such praying was never seen or heard before or since in London streets. A profane person ran one day out of the crowd, and hung about a priest's neck, where the beads should be, a string of puddings; but they whipped him, and prayed on. Surely, God would hear the cry of his people.

In the midst of the suspense the papal chair fell vacant again. The pontificate of Marcellus lasted three weeks, and Pole a third time offered himself to the suffrages of the cardinals. The courts were profuse of compliments as before. Noailles presented him with a note from Montmorency, containing assurances of the infinite desire of the King of France for the success of so holy a person. Philip wrote to Rome in his behalf, and Mary condescended to ask for the support of the French cardinals. But the fair speeches, as before, were but trifling. The choice fell on Pole's personal enemy, Cardinal Caraffa, who was French alike in heart and brain.

The choice of a pope, however, would signify little, if only the child could be born; but where was the child? The queen put it off strangely. The conference could be delayed no longer. It opened without the intended makeweight, and the court of France was less inclined to make concessions for a peace. The delay began to tell on the bourse at Antwerp.

The Fuggers and the Schertzes drew their purse-strings, and made difficulties in lending more money to the emperor. The plenipotentiaries had to separate after a few meetings, having effected nothing, to the especial mortification of Philip and Mary, who looked to the pacification to enable them to cure England of its unruly humours. The Duke of Alva (so rumour insisted) was to bring across the Spanish troops which were in the Low Countries, take possession of London, and force the parliament into submission. The English were to be punished, for the infinite insolences in which they had indulged towards Philip's retinue, by being compelled, whether they liked it or not, to bestow upon him the crown.

But the peace could not be, nor could the child be born; and the impression grew daily that the queen had not been pregnant at all. Mary herself, who had been borne forward to this, the crisis of her fortunes, on a tide of success, now suddenly found her exulting hopes closing over. From confidence she fell into anxiety, from anxiety into fear, from fear into wildness and despondency. She vowed that with the restoration of the estates, she would rebuild the abbeys at her own cost. In vain. Her women now understood her condition; she was sick of a mortal disease; but they durst not tell her; and she whose career had been painted out to her by the legate, as especial and supernatural, looked only for supernatural causes of her present state. Throughout May she remained in her apartments waiting – waiting – in passionate restlessness. With stomach swollen, and features shrunk and haggard, she would sit upon the floor, with her knees drawn up to her face, in an agony of doubt; and in mockery of her wretchedness, letters were again strewed about the place by an invisible agency, telling her that she was loathed by her people. She imagined they would rise again in her defence. But if they rose again, it would be to drive her and her husband from the country.

After the mysterious quickening on the legate's salutation, she could not doubt that her hopes had been at one time well founded; but for some fault, some error in herself, God had delayed the fulfilment of his promise. And what could that crime be? The accursed thing was still in the realm. She had been raised up, like the judges in Israel, for the extermination of God's enemies; and she had smitten but a few here and there, when, like the evil spirits, their name was legion. She had before sent orders round among the magistrates, to have their eyes upon them. On the 24th of May, when her distraction was at its height, she wrote a circular to quicken the over-languid zeal of the bishops.

"Right Reverend Father in God," it ran, "We greet you well; and where of late we addressed our letters unto the justices of the peace, within every of the counties within this our realm, whereby, amongst other good instructions given therein for the good order of the country about, they are willed to have special regard to such disordered persons as, forgetting their duty to Almighty God and us, do lean to any erroneous and heretical opinions; whom, if they cannot by good admonition and fair means reform, they are willed to deliver unto the ordinary, to be by him charitably travelled withal, and removed, if it may be, from their naughty opinions; or else, if they continue obstinate, to be ordered according to the laws provided in that behalf: understanding now, to our no little marvel, that divers of the said misordered persons, being, by the justices of the peace, for their contempt and obstinacy, brought to the ordinary, to be used as is aforesaid, are either refused to be received at their hands, or, if they be received, are neither so travelled with as Christian charity requireth, nor yet proceeded withal according to the order of justice, but are suffered to continue in their errors, to the dishonour of Almighty God, and dangerous example of others; like as we find this matter very strange, so have we thought convenient both to signify this our knowledge, and therewithal also to admonish you to have in this behalf such regard henceforth unto the office of a good pastor and bishop, as where any such offenders shall be, by the said justices of the peace, brought unto you, ye do use your good wisdom and discretion in procuring to remove them from their errors if it may be, or else in proceeding against them, if they continue obstinate, according to the order of the laws, so as, through your good furtherance, both God's glory may be the better advanced, and the commonwealth more quietly governed."

Under the fresh impulse of this letter, fifty persons were put to death at the stake in the three ensuing months, – in the diocese of London, under Bonner; in the diocese of Rochester, under Maurice Griffin; in the diocese of Canterbury, where Pole, the archbishop designate, so soon as Cranmer should be despatched, governed through Harpsfeld, the archdeacon, and Thornton, the suffragan bishop of Dover. Of these sacrifices, which were distinguished all of them by a uniformity of quiet heroism in the sufferers, that of Cardmaker, prebendary of Wells, calls most for notice.

The people, whom the cruelty of the Catholic party was reconverting to the Reformation with a rapidity like that produced by the gift of tongues on the day of Pentecost, looked on the martyrs as soldiers are looked at who are called to accomplish, with the sacrifice of their lives, some great service for their country. Cardmaker, on his first examination, had turned his back and flinched. But the consciousness of shame, and the example of others, gave him back his courage; he was called up again under the queen's mandate, condemned, and brought out on the 30th of May, to suffer at Smithfield, with an upholsterer named Warne. The sheriffs produced the pardons. Warne, without looking at them, undressed at once, and went to the stake; Cardmaker "remained long talking;" "the people in a marvellous dump of sadness, thinking he would recant." He turned away at last, and knelt, and prayed; but he had still his clothes on; "there was no semblance of burning;" and the crowd continued nervously agitated, till he rose and threw off his cloak. "Then, seeing this, contrary to their fearful expectations, as men delivered out of great doubt, they cried out for joy with so great a shout as hath not been lightly heard a greater, God be praised; the Lord strengthen thee, Cardmaker. The Lord Jesus receive thy spirit." Every martyr's trial was a battle; every constant death was a defeat of the common enemy; and the instinctive consciousness that truth was asserting itself in suffering, converted the natural emotion of horror into admiring pride.

Yet, for the great purpose of the court, the burnt-offerings were ineffectual as the prayers of the priests. The queen was allowed to persuade herself that she had mistaken her time by two months; and to this hope she clung herself, so long as the hope could last: but among all other persons concerned, scarcely one was any longer under a delusion; and the clear-eyed Renard lost no time in laying the position of affairs before his master.

The marriage of Elizabeth and Philibert had hung fire, from the invincible unwillingness on the part of Mary to pardon or in any way recognise her sister; and as long as there was a hope of a child, she had not perhaps been pressed about it; but it was now absolutely necessary to do something, and violent measures towards the princess were more impossible than ever.

"The entire future," wrote Renard to the emperor, on the 27th of June, "turns on the accouchement of the queen; of which, however, there are no signs. If all goes well, the state of feeling in the country will improve. If she is in error, I foresee convulsions and disturbances such as no pen can describe. The succession to the crown is so unfortunately hampered, that it must fall to Elizabeth, and with Elizabeth there will be a religious revolution. The clergy will be put down, the Catholics persecuted, and there will be such revenge for the present proceedings as the world has never seen. I know not whether the king's person is safe; and the scandals and calumnies which the heretics are spreading about the queen are beyond conception. Some say that she has never been *enceinte*; some repeat that there will be a supposititious child, and that there would have been less delay could a child have been found that would answer the purpose. The looks of men are grown strange and impenetrable; those in whose loyalty I had most dependence I have now most reason to doubt. Nothing is certain, and I am more bewildered than ever at the things which I see going on around me. There is neither government, nor justice, nor order; nothing but audacity and malice."

The faint hopes which Renard expressed speedily vanished, and every one but the queen herself not only knew that she had no child at present, but that she never could have a child – that her days were numbered, and that if the Spaniards intended to secure the throne they must obtain it by other means than the order of inheritance. Could the war be brought to an end, Mary might live long enough to give her husband an opportunity of attempting violence; but of peace there was no immediate prospect, and it remained for the present to make the most of Elizabeth. Setting her marriage aside, it was doubtful whether the people would permit her longer confinement after the queen's disappointment; and, willingly or unwillingly, Mary must be forced to receive her at court again.

The princess was still at Woodstock, where she had remained for a year, under the harsh surveillance of Sir Henry Bedingfield. Lord William Howard's visit may have consoled her with the knowledge that she was not forgotten by the nobility; but her health had suffered from her long imprisonment, and the first symptom of an approaching change in her position was the appearance of the queen's physician to take charge of her.

A last effort was made to betray her into an acknowledgment of guilt. "A secret friend" entreated her to "submit herself to the queen's mercy." Elizabeth saw the snare. She would not ask for mercy, she said, where she had committed no offence; if she was guilty, she desired justice, not mercy; and she knew well she would have found none, could evidence have been produced against her: but she thanked God she was in no danger of being proved guilty; she wished she was as safe from secret enemies.

But the plots for despatching her, if they had ever existed, were laid aside; she was informed that her presence was required at Hampton Court. The rumour of her intended release spread abroad, and sixty gentlemen, who had once belonged to her suite, met her on the way at Colebrook, in the hope that they might return to attendance upon her; but their coming was premature; she was still treated as a prisoner, and they were ordered off in the queen's name.

On her arrival at Hampton Court, however, the princess

felt that she had recovered her freedom. She was received by Lord William Howard. The courtiers hurried to her with their congratulations, and Howard dared and provoked the resentment of the king and queen by making them kneel and kiss her hand. Mary could not bring herself at first to endure an interview. The Bishop of Winchester came to her on the queen's behalf, to repeat the advice which had been given to her at Woodstock, and to promise pardon if she would ask for it.

Elizabeth had been resolute when she was alone and friendless, she was not more yielding now. She repeated that she had committed no offence, and therefore required no forgiveness; she had rather lie in prison all her life than confess when there was nothing to be confessed.

The answer was carried to Mary, and the day after the bishop came again. "The queen marvelled," he said, "that she would so stoutly stand to her innocence;" if she called herself innocent, she implied that she had been "unjustly imprisoned;" if she expected her liberty "she must tell another tale."

But the causes which had compelled the court to send for her, forbade them equally to persist in an impotent persecution. They had desired only to tempt her into admissions which they could plead in justification for past or future severities. They had failed, and they gave way.

A week later, on an evening in the beginning of July, Lady Clarence, Mary's favourite attendant, brought a message, that the queen was expecting her sister in her room. The princess was led across the garden in the dusk, and introduced by a back staircase into the royal apartments. Almost two years had elapsed since the sisters had last met, when Mary hid the hatred which was in her heart behind a veil of kindness.

119

There was no improvement of feeling, but the necessity of circumstances compelled the form of reconciliation.

Elizabeth dropped on her knees. "God preserve your majesty," she said; "you will find me as true a subject to your majesty as any; whatever has been reported of me, you shall not find it otherwise."

"You will not confess," the queen said; "you stand to your truth: I pray God it may so fall out."

"If it does not," said Elizabeth, "I desire neither favour nor pardon at your hands."

"Well," Mary bitterly answered, "you persevere in your truth stiffly; belike you will not confess that you have been wrongly punished?"

"I must not say so, your majesty," Elizabeth replied.

"Belike you will to others?" said the queen.

"No, please your majesty," answered the princess. "I have borne the burden, and I must bear it. I pray your majesty to have a good opinion of me, and to think me your true subject, not only from the beginning but while life lasteth."

The queen did not answer, she muttered only in Spanish, "*Sabe Dios*," "God knows," and Elizabeth withdrew.

It was said that, during the interview, Philip was concealed behind a curtain, anxious for a sight of the captive damsel whose favour with the people was such a perplexity to him.

At this time, Elizabeth was beautiful; her haughty features were softened by misfortune; and as it is certain that Philip, when he left England, gave special directions for her good treatment, so it is possible that he may have envied the fortune which he intended for the Prince of Savoy; and the scheme which he afterwards attempted to execute, of making her his own wife on the queen's death, may have then suggested itself to him as a solution of the English difficulty. The magnificent girl, who was already the idol of the country, must have presented an emphatic contrast with the lean, childless, haggard, forlorn Mary; and he may easily have allowed his fancy to play with a pleasant temptation. If it was so, Philip was far too careless of the queen's feelings to conceal his own. If it was not so, the queen's haunting consciousness of her unattractiveness must have been aggravated by the disappointment of her hopes, and she may have tortured herself with jealousy and suspicion.

At all events, Mary could not overcome her aversion. Elizabeth was set at liberty, but she was not allowed to remain at the court. She returned to Ashridge, to be pursued, even there, with petty annoyances. Her first step when she was again at home was to send for her friend Mrs. Ashley; the queen instantly committed Mrs. Ashley to the Fleet, and sent three other officers of her sister's household to the Tower; while a number of gentlemen suspected of being her adherents, who had remained in London beyond their usual time of leaving for the country, were ordered imperiously to their estates.

But neither impatience nor violence could conceal the fatal change which had passed over Mary's prospects. Not till the end of July could she part finally from her hopes. Then, at last, the glittering dream was lost for the waking truth; then at once from the imagination of herself as the virgin bride who was to bear a child for the recovery of a lost world, she was precipitated into the poor certainty that she was a blighted and a dying woman. Sorrow was heaped on sorrow; Philip would stay with her no longer. His presence was required on the continent, where his father was about to anticipate the death which he knew to be near, and, after forty years of battling with the stormy waters, to collect himself for the last great change in the calm of a monastery in Spain.

It was no new intention. For years the emperor had been in the habit of snatching intervals of retreat; for years he had made up his mind to relinquish at some time the labours of life before relinquishing life itself. The vanities of sovereignty had never any particular charm for Charles V.; he was not a man who cared "to monarchise and kill with looks," or who could feel a pang at parting with the bauble of a crown; and when the wise world cried out in their surprise, and strained their fancies for the cause of conduct which seemed so strange to them, they forgot that princes who reign to labour, grow weary like the peasant of the burden of daily toil.

Many influences combined to induce Charles to delay no longer in putting his resolution in effect.

The Cortes were growing impatient at the prolonged absence both of himself and Philip, and the presence of the emperor, although in retirement, would give pleasure to the Spanish people. His health was so shattered, that each winter had been long expected to be his last; and although he would not flinch from work as long as he was required at his post, there was nothing to detain Philip any more in England, unless, or until, the succession could be placed on another footing. To continue there the husband of a childless queen, with authority limited to a form, and with no recognised interest beyond the term of his wife's life, was no becoming position for the heir of the throne of Spain, of Naples, the Indies, and the Low Countries.

Philip was therefore now going. He concealed his intention till it was betrayed by the departure of one Spanish nobleman after another. The queen became nervous and agitated, and at last he was forced to avow part of the truth. He told her that his father wanted to see him, but that his absence would not be extended beyond a fortnight or three weeks; she should go with him to Dover, and, if she desired, she could wait there for his return. Her consent was obtained by the mild deceit, and it was considered afterwards that the journey to Dover might be too much for her, and the parting might take place at Greenwich.

On the 3rd of August, the king and queen removed for a few days from Hampton Court to Oatlands; on the way Mary received consolation from a poor man who met her on crutches, and was cured of his lameness by looking on her.

On the 26th, the royal party came down the river in their barge, attended by the legate; they dined at Westminster on their way to Greenwich, and as rumour had said that Mary was dead, she was carried through the city in an open litter, with the king and the cardinal at her side. To please Philip, or to please the people, Elizabeth was invited to the court before the king's departure; but she was sent by water to prevent a demonstration, while the archers of the guard who attended on the queen, were in corslet and morion.

On the 28th, Philip went. Parliament was to sit again in October. It would then be seen whether anything more could be done about the succession. On the consent or refusal of the legislature his future measures would depend. To the queen he left particular instructions, which he afterwards repeated in writing, to show favour to Elizabeth; and doubting how far he could rely upon Mary, he gave a similar charge to such of his own suite as he left behind him. Could he obtain it, he would take the princess's crown for himself; should he fail, he might marry her; or should this too be impossible, he would win her gratitude, and support her title against the dangerous competition of the Queen of Scots and Dauphiness of France.

On these terms the pair who had been brought together with so much difficulty separated after a little more than a year. The cardinal composed a passionate prayer for the queen's use during her husband's absence. It is to be hoped that she was spared the sight of a packet of letters soon after intercepted by the French, in which her husband and her husband's countrymen expressed their opinions of the marriage and its consequences. The truth, however, became known in England, although in a form under which the queen could turn from it as a calumny.

Before the meeting of parliament, a letter was published, addressed to the Lords of the Council, by a certain John Bradford. The writer accounted for his knowledge of the secrets which he had to tell, by saying that he had lived in the household of one of the Spanish noblemen who were in attendance on Philip; that he had learnt the language unknown to his master, and had thus overheard unguarded conversations. He had read letters addressed to Philip, and letters written by him and by his confidential friends; and he was able to say, as a thing heard with his own ears, and seen with his own eyes, that the "Spaniards minded nothing less than the subversion of the English commonwealth." In fact, he repeated the rumours of the summer, only more circumstantially, and with fuller details. Under pretence of improving the fortifications, Philip intended to obtain command of the principal harbours and ports; he would lay cannon on the land side, and gradually bring in Spanish troops, the queen playing into his hands; and as soon as peace could be made with France, he would have the command of the fleet and the sea, and could do what he pleased.

"I saw," the writer continued, "letters sent from the emperor, wherein was contained these privities, – that the king should make his excuse to the queen that he would go to see his father in Flanders, and that immediately he would return – seeing the good simple queen is so jealous over my son. (I term it," said Bradford, "as the letter doth.") "We," said the emperor, "shall make her agree unto all our requests before his return, or else keep him exercised in our affairs till we may prevail with the council, who, doubtless, will be won with fair promises and great gifts, politicly placed in time." "In other letters I have read the cause disputed, that the queen is bound by the laws of God to endue her husband in all her goods and possessions, so far as in her lieth; and they think she will do it indeed to the uttermost of her power. No man can think evil of the queen, though she be somewhat moved when such things are beaten into her head with gentlemen; but whether the crown belongs to the queen or the realm, the Spaniards know not, nor care not, though the queen, to her damnation, disherit the right heir apparent, or break her father's entail, made by the whole consent of the realm, which neither she nor the realm can justly alter."

Struggle as the queen might against such a representation of her husband's feelings towards her, it was true that he had left her with a promise to return; and the weeks went, and he did not come, and no longer spoke of coming. The abdication of the emperor would keep him from her, at least, till the end of the winter. And news came soon which was harder still to bear; news, that he, whom she had been taught to regard as made in the image of our Saviour, was unfaithful to his marriage vows, Bradford had spoken generally of the king's vulgar amours; other accounts convinced her too surely that he was consoling himself for his long purgatory in England, by miscellaneous licentiousness. Philip was gross alike in all his appetites; bacon fat was the favourite food with which he gorged himself to illness; his intrigues were on the same level of indelicacy, and his unhappy wife was forced to know that he preferred the society of abandoned women of the lowest class to hers.

The French ambassador describes her as distracted with wretchedness, speaking to no one except the legate. The legate was her only comfort; the legate and the thing which she called religion.

Deep in the hearts of both queen and cardinal lay the conviction that if she would please God, she must avoid the sin of Saul. Saul had spared the Amalekites, and God had turned his face from him. God had greater enemies in England than the Amalekites. Historians have affected to exonerate Pole from the crime of the Marian persecution; although, without the legate's sanction, not a bishop in England could have raised a finger, not a bishop's court could have been opened to try a single heretic. If not with Pole, with whom did the guilt rest? Gardiner was jointly responsible for the commencement, but after the first executions, Gardiner interfered no further; he died, and the bloody scenes continued. Philip's confessor protested; Philip himself left the country; Renard and Charles were never weary of advising moderation, except towards those who were politically dangerous. Bonner was an instrument whose zeal more than once required the goad; and Mary herself, when she came to the throne, was so little cruel, that she would have spared even Northumberland himself. When the persecution assumed its ferocious aspect, she was exclusively under the direction of the dreamer who believed that he was born for England's regeneration. All evidence concurs to show that, after Philip's departure, Cardinal

Pole was the single adviser on whom Mary relied. Is it to be supposed that, in the horrible crusade which thenceforward was the business of her life, the papal legate, the sovereign director of the ecclesiastical administration of the realm, was not consulted, or, if consulted, that he refused his sanction? But it is not a question of conjecture or probability. From the legate came the first edict for the episcopal inquisition; under the legate every bishop held his judicial commission; while, if Smithfield is excepted, the most frightful scenes in the entire frightful period were witnessed under the shadow of his own metropolitan cathedral. His apologists have thrown the blame on his archdeacon and his suffragan: the guilt is not with the instrument, but with the hand which holds it. An admiring biographer has asserted that the cruelties at Canterbury preceded the cardinal's consecration as archbishop, and the biographer has been copied by Dr. Lingard. The historian and his authority have exceeded the limits of permitted theological misrepresentation. The administration of the see belonged to Pole as much before his consecration as after it; but it will be seen that eighteen men and women perished at the stake in the town of Canterbury alone, – besides those who were put to death in other parts of the diocese – and five were starved to death in the gaol there – after the legate's installation. He was not cruel; but he believed that, in the catalogue of human iniquities, there were none greater than the denial of the Roman Catholic Faith, or the rejection of the Roman bishop's supremacy; and that he himself was chosen by Providence for the re-establishment of both. Mary was driven to madness by the disappointment of the grotesque imaginations with which he had inflated her; and where two such persons were invested by the circumstances of the time with irresponsible power, there is no occasion to look further for the explanation of the dreadful events of the three ensuing years.

## THE BURNINGS OF RIDLEY AND LATIMER

A commission was appointed by Pole in September, consisting of Brookes, Bishop of Gloucester, Holyman, Bishop of Bristol, and White, Bishop of Lincoln, to try Cranmer, Ridley, and Latimer, for obstinate heresy. The first trial had been irregular; the country was then unreconciled. The sentence which had been passed therefore was treated as non-existent, and the tedious forms of the papacy continued still to throw a shield round the archbishop.

On Saturday, the 7th of September, the commissioners took their places under the altar of St. Mary's Church, at Oxford. The Bishop of Gloucester sat as president, Doctors Story and Martin appeared as proctors for the queen, and Cranmer was brought in under the custody of the city guard, in a black gown and leaning on a stick.

"Thomas, Archbishop of Canterbury," cried an officer of the court, "appear here, and make answer to that which shall be laid to thy charge; that is to say, for blasphemy, incontinency, and heresy; make answer to the Bishop of Gloucester, representing his holiness the pope."

The archbishop approached the bar, bent his head and uncovered to Story and Martin, who were present in behalf of the crown, then drew himself up, put on his cap again, and stood fronting Brookes. "My lord," he said, "I mean no contempt to your person, which I could have honoured as well as any of the others; but I have sworn never to admit the authority of the Bishop of Rome in England, and I must keep my oath."

The president remonstrated, but without effect, and then proceeded to address the archbishop, who remained covered:

"My lord, we are come hither at this present to you, not intruding ourselves by our own authority, but sent by commission, as you know, by the pope's holiness partly; partly from the king's and queen's most excellent majesties; not utterly to your discomfort, but rather to your comfort if you will yourself. For we are come not to judge you immediately, but to put you in remembrance of that which you have been partly judged of before, and shall be thoroughly judged of ere long.

"Neither our coming or commission is to dispute with you, but to examine you in matters which you have already disputed in, taught, and written; and of your resolute answers in those points and others, to make relation to them that shall give sentence on you. If you, of your part, be moved to come to a uniformity, then shall not only we take joy of our examination, but also they that have sent us. Remember yourself then, *unde excideris*, from whence you have fallen. You have fallen from the unity of your mother, the Holy Catholic Church, and that by open schism. You have fallen from the true and received faith of the same Catholic Church, and that by open heresy. You have fallen from your fidelity and promise towards God, in breaking your orders and vow of chastity, and that by open apostasy. You have fallen from your fidelity and promise towards God's vicar-general, the pope, in breaking your oath made to his holiness at your consecration, and that by open perjury. You have fallen from your fidelity and allegiance towards God's magistrate, your prince and sovereign lady the queen, and that by open treason, whereof you are already attainted and convicted. Remember, *unde excideris*, from whence you have fallen, and in what danger you have fallen.

"You were sometime, as I and other poor men, in mean estate. God hath called you from better to better, from higher to higher, and never gave you over till he made you, *legatum natum*, Metropolitan Archbishop, Primate of England. Who was more earnest then in defence of the real presence of Christ's body and blood in the sacrament of the altar than ye were? Then was your candle shining to be a light to all the world, set on high on a pinnacle. But after you began to fall from the unity of the Catholic Church by open schism, and would no longer acknowledge the supremacy of the pope's holiness by God's word and ordinance; – and that by occasion, that you, in whose hands then rested the sum of all, being primate, as was aforesaid, would not, according to your high vocation, stoutly withstand the most ungodly and unlawful request of your prince touching his divorce, as that blessed martyr, St. Thomas of Canterbury, sometime your predecessor, did withstand the unlawful requests of the prince of his time, but would still not only yield and bear with things not to be borne withal, but also set a-flame the fire already kindled – then your perfections diminished; then began you, for your own part, to fancy unlawful liberty. Then decayed your conscience of your former faith, your former promise, the vow of chastity and discipline after the order of priesthood; and when good conscience was once cast off, then followed after, as St. Paul noteth, a shipwreck in the faith. Then fell you from the faith, and out of the Catholic Church, as out of a sure ship, into a sea of dangerous desperation; for out of the church, to say with St. Cyprian, there is no hope of salvation at all. To be brief; when you had forsaken God, his Spouse, his faith, and fidelity to them both, then God forsook you; and as the apostle writeth of the ingrate philosophers, delivered you up *in reprobum sensum,* and suffered you to fall from one inconvenience to another, as from perjury into schism, from schism into a kind of apostasy, from apostasy into heresy, from heresy into traitory, and so, in conclusion, from traitory into the highest displeasure and worthiest indignation of your most benign and gracious queen."

When the bishop ceased, the crown proctors rose, and demanded justice against the prisoner in the names of the king and queen.

"My lord," Cranmer replied, "I do not acknowledge this session of yours, nor yet yourself my mislawful judge; neither would I have appeared this day before you, but that I was brought hither; and therefore here I openly renounce you as my judge, protesting that my meaning is not to make any answer as in a lawful judgment, for then I would be silent; but only for that I am bound in conscience to answer every man of that hope which I have in Jesus Christ."

He then knelt, and turning towards the west with his back to the court and the altar, he said the Lord's Prayer. After which, he rose, repeated the creed, and said –

"This I do profess as touching my faith, and make my protestation, which I desire you to note; I will never consent that the Bishop of Rome shall have any jurisdiction in this realm."

"Mark, Master Cranmer," interrupted Martin, "you refuse and deny him by whose laws you do remain in life, being otherwise attainted of high treason, and but a dead man by the laws of the realm."

"I protest before God I was no traitor," said the archbishop. "I will never consent to the Bishop of Rome, for then I should give myself to the devil. I have made an oath to the king, and I must obey the king by God's law. By the Scripture, the king is chief, and no foreign person in his own realm above him. The pope is contrary to the crown. I cannot obey both, for no man can serve two masters at once. You attribute the keys to the pope and the sword to the king. I say the king hath both."

Continuing the same argument, the archbishop entered at length into the condition of the law and the history of the Statutes of Provisors and Premunire: he showed that the constitution of the country was emphatically independent, and he maintained that no English subject could swear obedience to a foreign power without being involved in perjury.

The objection was set aside, and the subject of oaths was an opportunity for a taunt, which the queen's proctors did not overlook. Cranmer had unwillingly accepted the archbishopric when the Act of Appeals was pending, and when the future relations of England with the See of Rome, and the degree of authority which (if any) the pope was to retain, were uncertain. In taking the usual oaths, therefore, by the advice of lawyers, he made an especial and avowed reservation of his duty to the crown; and this so-called perjury Martin now flung in his teeth.

"It pleased the king's highness," Cranmer replied, "many and sundry times to talk with me of the matter. I declared that, if I accepted the office of archbishop, I must receive it at the pope's hands, which I neither would nor could do, for his highness was the only supreme governor of this church in England. Perceiving that I could not be brought to acknowledge the authority of the Bishop of Rome, the king called Doctor Oliver and other civil lawyers, and devised with them how he might bestow it on me, enforcing me nothing against my conscience, who informed him I might do it by way of protestation. I said, I did not acknowledge the Bishop of Rome's authority further than as it agreed with the word of God, and that it might be lawful for me at all times to speak against him; and my protestation did I cause to be enrolled, and there I think it remaineth."

"Let your protestation, with the rest of your talk, give judgment against you," answered Martin. "*Hinc prima mali labes*: of that your execrable perjury, and the king's coloured and too shamefully suffered adultery, came heresy and all mischief into the realm."

The special charges were then proceeded with.

In reply to a series of questions, the archbishop said, that he had been twice married – once before, and once after he was in orders. In the time of Henry, he had kept his wife secretly, "affirming that it was better for him to have his own wife, than to do like other priests, having the wives of others;" and he was not ashamed of what he had done.

He admitted his writings upon the Eucharist; he avowed the authorship of the Catechism, of the Articles, and of a book against the Bishop of Winchester; and these books, and his conduct generally as Archbishop of Canterbury, he maintained and defended. His replies were entered by a notary, to be transmitted to the pope, and for the present the business of the court with him was over.

"Who can stay him that willingly runneth into perdition?" said Brookes. "Who can save that will be lost? God would have you to be saved, and you refuse it."

The archbishop was cited to appear at Rome within eighty days to answer to the charges which would there be laid against him; and in order that he might be able to obey the summons he was returned to his cell in Bocardo prison, and kept there in strict confinement.

Ridley and Latimer came next, and over them the papal mantle flung no protection.

They had been prisoners now for more than two years. What Latimer's occupation had been for all that time, little remains to show, except three letters: one, of but a few lines, was to a Mrs. Wilkinson, thanking her for some act of kindness: another, was a general exhortation to "all unfeigned lovers of God's truth," to be constant in their faith: the third, and most noteworthy, was to some one who had an opportunity of escaping from arrest, and probable martyrdom, by a payment of money, and who doubted whether he might lawfully avail himself of the chance: there was no question of recantation; a corrupt official was ready to accept a bribe and ask no questions.

Latimer had not been one of those fanatics who thought it a merit to go in the way of danger and court persecution; but in this present case he shared the misgiving of his correspondent, and did "highly allow his judgment in that he thought it not lawful to redeem himself from the crown, unless he would exchange glory for shame, and his inheritance for a mess of pottage."

"We were created," Latimer said, "to set forth God's glory all the days of our life, which we, as unthankful sinners, have forgotten to do, as we ought, all our days hitherto; and now God, by affliction, doth offer us good occasion to perform one day of our life, our duty. If any man perceive his faith not to abide the fire, let such an one with weeping buy his liberty until he hath obtained more strength, lest the gospel suffer by him some shameful recantation. Let the dead bury the dead. Do you embrace Christ's cross, and Christ shall embrace you. The peace of God be with you for ever."

Ridley's pen had been more busy: he had written a

lamentation over the state of England; he had written a farewell letter, taking leave of his friends, and taking leave of life, which, clouded as it was, his sunny nature made it hard to part from: he had written comfort to the afflicted for the gospel, and he had addressed a passionate appeal to the Temporal Lords to save England from the false shepherds who were wasting the flock of Christ. But both he and Latimer had looked death steadily in the face for two years, expecting it every day or hour. It was now come.

On the 30th of September, the three bishops took their seats in the Divinity school. Ridley was led in for trial, and the legate's commission was read, empowering them to try him for the opinions which he had expressed in the disputation at Oxford the year before, and "elsewhere in the time of perdition." They were to degrade him from the priesthood if he persisted in his heresies, and deliver him over to the secular arm.

On being first brought before the court, Ridley stood bareheaded. At the names of the cardinal and the pope, he put on his cap, like Cranmer, declining to acknowledge their authority. But his scruples were treated less respectfully than the archbishop's. He was ordered to take it off, and when he refused, it was removed by a beadle.

He was then charged with having denied transubstantiation, and the propitiatory sacrifice of the mass, and was urged at length to recant. His opinions on the real presence were peculiar. Christ, he said, was not the sacrament, but was really and truly in the sacrament, as the Holy Ghost was with the water at baptism and yet was not the water. The subtlety of the position was perplexing, but the knot was cut by the crucial question, whether, after the consecration of the elements, the substance of bread and wine remained. He was allowed the night to consider his answer, but he left no doubt what that answer would be. "The bishops told him that they were not come to condemn him, their province was to condemn no one, but only to cut off the heretic from the church, for the temporal judge to deal with as he should think fit." The cowardly sophism had been heard too often. Ridley thanked the court "for their gentleness," "being the same which Christ had of the high priest:" "the high priest said it was not lawful for him to put any man to death, but committed Christ to Pilate; neither would suffer him to absolve Christ, though he sought all the means therefore that he might."

Ridley withdrew, and Latimer was then introduced – eighty years old now – dressed in an old threadbare gown of Bristol frieze, a handkerchief on his head with a night-cap over it, and over that again another cap, with two broad flaps buttoned under the chin. A leather belt was round his waist, to which a Testament was attached; his spectacles, without a case, hung from his neck. So stood the greatest man perhaps then living in the world, a prisoner on his trial, waiting to be condemned to death by men professing to be the ministers of God. As it was in the days of the prophets, so it was in the Son of man's days; as it was in the days of the Son of man, so was it in the Reformers' days; as it was in the days of the Reformers, so will it be to the end, so long and so far as a class of men are permitted to hold power, who call themselves the commissioned and authoritative teachers of truth. Latimer's trial was the counterpart of Ridley's: the charge was the same, and the result was the same, except that the stronger intellect vexed itself less with nice distinctions. Bread was bread, said Latimer, and wine was wine; there was a change in the sacrament, it was true, but the change was not in the nature, but the dignity. He too was reprieved for the day. The following morning, the court sat in St. Mary's Church, with the authorities of town and university, heads of houses, mayor, aldermen, and sheriff. The prisoners were brought to the bar. The same questions were asked, the same answers were returned, and sentence was pronounced upon them, as heretics obstinate and incurable.

Execution did not immediately follow. The convictions for which they were about to die had been adopted by both of them comparatively late in life. The legate would not relinquish the hope of bringing them back into the superstition in which they had been born, and had lived so long; and Soto, a Spanish friar, who was teaching divinity at Oxford in the place of Peter Martyr, was set to work on them.

But one of them would not see him, and on the other he could make no impression. Those whom God had cast away, thought Pole, were not to be saved by man; and the 16th of October was fixed upon as the day on which they were to suffer. Ridley had been removed from Bocardo, and was under the custody of the mayor, a man named Irish, whose wife was a bigoted and fanatical Catholic. On the evening of the 15th there was a supper at the mayor's house, where some members of Ridley's family were permitted to be present. He talked cheerfully of his approaching "marriage;" his brother-in-law promised to be in attendance, and, if possible, to bring with him his wife, Ridley's sister. Even the hard eyes of Mrs. Irish were softened to tears, as she listened and thought of what was coming. The brother-in-law offered to sit up through the night, but Ridley said there was no occasion; he "minded to go to bed, and sleep as quietly as ever he did in his life." In the morning he wrote a letter to the queen. As Bishop of London he had granted renewals of certain leases, on which he had received fines. Bonner had

137

refused to recognise them, and he entreated the queen, for Christ's sake, either that the leases should be allowed, or that some portion of his own confiscated property might be applied to the repayment of the tenants. The letter was long; by the time it was finished, the sheriff's officers were probably in readiness.

The place selected for the burning was outside the north wall of the town, a short stone's throw from the southward corner of Balliol College, and about the same distance from Bocardo prison, from which Cranmer was intended to witness his friends' sufferings.

Lord Williams of Thame was on the spot by the queen's order; and the city guard were under arms to prevent disturbance. Ridley appeared first, walking between the mayor and one of the aldermen. He was dressed in a furred black gown, "such as he was wont to wear being bishop," a furred velvet tippet about his neck, and a velvet cap. He had trimmed his beard, and had washed himself from head to foot; a man evidently nice in his appearance, a gentleman, and liking to be known as such. The way led under the windows of Bocardo, and he looked up; but Soto, the friar, was with the archbishop, making use of the occasion, and Ridley did not see him. In turning round, however, he saw Latimer coming up behind him in the frieze coat, with the cap and handkerchief – the workday costume unaltered, except that under his cloak, and reaching to his feet, the old man wore a long new shroud.

"Oh! be ye there?" Ridley exclaimed.

"Yea," Latimer answered. "Have after as fast as I can follow."

Ridley ran to him and embraced him. "Be of good heart, brother," he said. "God will either assuage the flame, or else strengthen us to abide it." They knelt and prayed together, and then exchanged a few words in a low voice, which were not overheard.

Lord Williams, the vice-chancellor, and the doctors were seated on a form close to the stake. A sermon was preached, "a scant one," "of scarce a quarter of an hour;" and then Ridley begged that for Christ's sake he might say a few words.

Lord Williams looked to the doctors, one of whom started from his seat, and laid his hand on Ridley's lips –

"Recant," he said, "and you may both speak and live."

"So long as the breath is in my body," Ridley answered, "I will never deny my Lord Christ and his known truth. God's will be done in me. I commit our cause," he said, in a loud voice, turning to the people, "to Almighty God, who shall indifferently judge all."

The brief preparations were swiftly made. Ridley gave his gown and tippet to his brother-in-law, and distributed remembrances among those who were nearest to him. To Sir Henry Lee he gave a new groat, to others he gave handkerchiefs, nutmegs, slices of ginger, his watch, and miscellaneous trinkets; "some plucked off the points of his hose;" "happy," it was said, "was he that might get any rag of him."

Latimer had nothing to give. He threw off his cloak, stood bolt upright in his shroud, and the friends took their places on either side of the stake.

"O Heavenly Father," Ridley said, "I give unto thee most humble thanks, for that thou hast called me to be a professor of thee even unto death. Have mercy, O Lord, on this realm of England, and deliver the same from all her enemies."

A chain was passed round their bodies, and fastened with a staple.

A friend brought a bag of powder and hung it round Ridley's neck.

"I will take it to be sent of God," Ridley said. "Have you more, for my brother?"

"Yea, sir," the friend answered. "Give it him betimes then," Ridley replied, "lest ye be too late."

The fire was then brought. To the last moment, Ridley was distressed about the leases, and, bound as he was, he entreated Lord Williams to intercede with the queen about them.

"I will remember your suit," Lord Williams answered. The lighted torch was laid to the faggots. "Be of good comfort, Master Ridley," Latimer cried at the crackling of the flames; "Play the man: we shall this day light such a candle, by God's, grace, in England, as I trust shall never be put out."

"*In manus tuas, Domine, commendo spiritum meum,*" cried Ridley. "*Domine, recipe spiritum meum.*"

"O Father of Heaven," said Latimer, on the other side, "receive my soul."

Latimer died first: as the flame blazed up about him, he bathed his hands in it, and stroked his face. The powder exploded, and he became instantly senseless.

His companion was less fortunate. The sticks had been piled too thickly over the gorse that was under them; the fire smouldered round his legs, and the sensation of suffering was unusually protracted. "I cannot burn," he called; "Lord have mercy on me; let the fire come to me; I cannot burn." His brother-in-law, with awkward kindness, threw on more wood, which only kept down the flame. At last some one lifted the pile with "a bill," and let in the air; the red tongues of fire shot up fiercely, Ridley wrested himself into the middle of them, and the powder did its work.

The horrible sight worked upon the beholders as it has worked since, and will work for ever, while the English nation survives – being, notwithstanding, as in justice to those who caused these accursed cruelties, must never be forgotten – a legitimate fruit of the superstition, that, in the eyes of the Maker of the world, an error of belief is the greatest of crimes; that while for all other sins there is forgiveness, a mistake in the intellectual intricacies of speculative opinion will be punished not with the brief agony of a painful death, but with tortures to which there shall be no end.

## THE MARTYRDOM OF CRANMER

On the 14th of December, a mock trial was instituted at Rome; the report of the examination at Oxford was produced, and counsel were heard on both sides, or so it was pretended. Paul IV. then pronounced the final sentence, that Thomas Cranmer, Archbishop of Canterbury, having been accused by his sovereigns of divers crimes and misdemeanours, it had been proved against him that he had followed the teachings of John Wicliff and Martin Luther of accursed memory; that he had published books containing matters of heresy, and still obstinately persisted in those his erroneous opinions: he was therefore declared to be anathema, to be deprived of his office, and having been degraded, he was to be delivered over to the secular arm.

There was some delay in sending the judgment to England. It arrived at the beginning of February, and on the 14th, Thirlby and Bonner went down to finish the work at Oxford. The court sat this time in Christ Church Cathedral. Cranmer was brought to the bar, and the papal sentence was read. The preamble declared that the cause had been heard with indifference, that the accused had been defended by an advocate, that witnesses had been examined for him, that he had been allowed every opportunity to answer for himself. "O Lord," he exclaimed, "what lies be these! that I, being in prison and never suffered to have counsel or advocate at home, should produce witness and appoint counsel at Rome; God must needs punish this shameless lying."

Silence would perhaps have been more dignified; to speak at all was an indication of infirmity. As soon as the reading was finished, the archbishop was formally arrayed in his robes, and when the decoration was completed, Bonner called out in exultation:

"This is the man that hath despised the pope's holiness, and now is to be judged by him; this is the man that hath pulled down so many churches, and now is come to be judged in a church; this is the man that hath contemned the blessed sacrament of the altar, and now is come to be condemned before that blessed sacrament hanging over the altar; this is the man that, like Lucifer, sat in the place of Christ upon an altar to judge others, and now is come before an altar to be judged himself."

Thirlby checked the insolence of his companion. The degradation was about to commence, when the archbishop drew from his sleeve an appeal "to the next Free General Council that should be called." It had been drawn after consultation with a lawyer, in the evident hope that it might save or prolong his life, and he attempted to present it to his judges. But he was catching at straws, as in his clearer judgment he would have known. Thirlby said sadly that the appeal could not be received; his orders were absolute to proceed.

The robes were stripped off in the usual way. The thin hair

was clipped. Bonner with his own hands scraped the finger points which had been touched with the oil of consecration; "Now are you lord no longer," he said, when the ceremony was finished. "All this needed not," Cranmer answered; "I had myself done with this gear long ago."

He was led off in a beadle's threadbare gown, and a tradesman's cap; and here for some important hours authentic account of him is lost. What he did, what he said, what was done or what was said to him, is known only in its results, or in Protestant tradition. Tradition said that he was taken from the cathedral to the house of the Dean of Christ Church, where he was delicately entertained, and worked upon with smooth words, and promises of life. "The noblemen," he was told, "bare him good-will; he was still strong, and might live many years, why should he cut them short?" The story may contain some elements of truth. But the same evening, certainly, he was again in his cell; and among the attempts to move him which can be authenticated, there was one of a far different kind; a letter addressed to him by Pole to bring him to a sense of his condition.

"Whosoever transgresseth, and abideth not in the doctrine of Christ," so the legate addressed a prisoner in the expectation of death, "hath not God. He that abideth in the doctrine of Christ, he hath both the Father and the Son. If there come any unto you and bring not this doctrine, receive him not into your house, neither bid him God speed; for he that biddeth him God speed is partaker of his evil deeds. There are some who tell me that, in obedience to this command, I ought not to address you, or to have any dealings with you, save the dealings of a judge with a criminal. But Christ came not to judge only, but also to save; I call upon you, not to enter into your house, for so I should make myself a partaker with you; my desire is only to bring you back to the church which you have deserted.

"You have corrupted Scripture, you have broken through the communion of saints, and now I tell you what you must do; I tell you, or rather not I, but Christ and the church through me. Did I follow my own impulse, or did I speak in my own name, I should hold other language; to you I should not speak at all; I would address myself only to God; I would pray him to let fall the fire of Heaven to consume you, and to consume with you the house into which you have entered in abandoning the church.

"You pretend that you have used no instruments but reason to lead men after you; what instrument did the devil use to seduce our parents in Paradise? you have followed the serpent; with guile you destroyed your king, the realm, and the church, and you have brought to perdition thousands of human souls.

"Compared with you, all others who have been concerned in these deeds of evil, are but objects of pity; many of them long resisted temptation, and yielded only to the seductions of your impious tongue; you made yourself a bishop – for what purpose, but to mock both God and man? Your first act was but to juggle with your king, and you were no sooner primate, than you plotted how you might break your oath to the Holy See; you took part in the counsels of the evil one, you made your home with the wicked, you sat in the seat of the scornful. You exhorted your king with your fine words, to put away his wife; you prated to him of his obligations to submit to the judgment of the church; and what has followed that unrighteous sentence? You parted the king from the wife with whom he had lived for twenty years; you parted him from the church, the common mother of the faithful; and thenceforth throughout the realm law has been trampled under foot, the people have been ground with tyranny, the churches pillaged, the nobility murdered one by the other.

"Therefore, I say, were I to make my own cries heard in heaven, I would pray God to demand at your hands the blood of his servants. Never had religion, never had the church of Christ a worse enemy than you have been; now therefore, when you are about to suffer the just reward of your deeds, think no more to excuse yourself; confess your sins, like the penitent thief upon the cross.

"Say not in your defence that you have done no violence, that you have been kind and gentle in your daily life. Thus I know men speak of you; but cheat not your conscience with so vain a plea. The devil, when called to answer for the souls that he has slain, may plead likewise that he did not desire their destruction; he thought only to make them happy, to give them pleasure, honour, riches – all things which their hearts desired. So did you with your king: you gave him the woman that he lusted after; you gave him the honour which was not his due, and the good things which were neither his nor yours; and, last and worst, you gave him poison, in covering his iniquities with a cloak of righteousness. Better, far better, you had offered him courtesans for companions; better you and he had been open thieves and robbers. Then he might have understood his crimes, and have repented of them; but you tempted him into the place where there is no repentance, no hope of salvation.

"Turn then yourself, and repent. See yourself as you are. Thus may you escape your prison. Thus may you flee out of the darkness wherein you have hid yourself. Thus may you come back to light and life, and earn for yourself God's forgiveness. I know not how to deal with you. Your examination at Oxford has but hardened you; yet the issue is with God. I at least can point out to you the way. If you, then, persist in your vain opinions, may God have mercy on you."

The legate, in his office of guide, then travelled the full round of controversy, through Catholic tradition, through the doctrine of the sacraments and of the real presence, where there is no need to follow him. At length he drew to his conclusion:

"You will plead Scripture to answer me. Are you so vain, then, are you so foolish, as to suppose that it has been left to you to find out the meaning of those Scriptures which have been in the hands of the fathers of the church for so many ages? Confess, confess that you have mocked God in denying that he is present on the altar; wash out your sins with tears; and in the abundance of your sorrow you may find pardon. May it be so. Even for the greatness of your crimes may it be so, that God may have the greater glory. You have not, like others, fallen through simplicity, or fallen through fear. You were corrupted, like the Jews, by earthly rewards and promises. For your own profit you denied the presence of your Lord, and you rebelled against his servant the pope. May you see your crimes. May you feel the greatness of your need of mercy. Now, even now, by my mouth, Christ offers you that mercy; and with the passionate hope which I am bound to feel for your salvation, I wait your answer to your Master's call."

The exact day on which this letter reached the archbishop is uncertain, but it was very near the period of his sentence. He had dared death bravely while it was distant; but he was physically timid; the near approach of the agony which he had witnessed in others unnerved him; and in a moment of mental and moral prostration Cranmer may well have looked in the mirror which Pole held up to him, and asked himself whether, after all, the being there described was his true image – whether it was himself as others saw him. A faith which had existed for centuries, a faith in which generation after generation have lived happy and virtuous lives; a faith in which all good men are agreed, and only the bad dispute – such a faith carries an evidence and a weight with it beyond what can be looked for in a creed reasoned out by individuals – a creed which had the ban upon it of inherited execration; which had been held in abhorrence once by him who was now called upon to die for it. Only fools and fanatics believe that they cannot be mistaken. Sick misgivings may have taken hold upon him in moments of despondency, whether, after all, the millions who received the Roman supremacy might not be more right than the thousands who denied it; whether the argument on the real presence, which had satisfied him for fifty years, might not be better founded than his recent doubts. It is not possible for a man of gentle and modest nature to feel himself the object of intense detestation without uneasy pangs; and as such thoughts came and went, a window might seem to open, through which there was a return to life and freedom. His trial was not greater than hundreds of others had borne, and would bear with constancy; but the temperaments of men are unequally constituted, and a subtle intellect and a sensitive organisation are not qualifications which make martyrdom easy.

Life, by the law of the church, by justice, by precedent, was given to all who would accept it on terms of submission. That the archbishop should be tempted to recant, with the resolution formed, notwithstanding, that he should still suffer, whether he yielded or whether he was obstinate, was a suspicion which his experience of the legate had not taught him to entertain.

So it was that Cranmer's spirit gave way, and he who had disdained to fly when flight was open to him, because he considered that, having done the most in establishing the Reformation, he was bound to face the responsibility of it, fell at last under the protraction of the trial.

The day of his degradation the archbishop had eaten little. In the evening he returned to his cell in a state of exhaustion: the same night, or the next day, he sent in his first submission, which was forwarded on the instant to the queen. It was no sooner gone than he recalled it, and then vacillating again, he drew a second, in slightly altered words, which he signed and did not recall. There had been a struggle in which the weaker nature had prevailed, and the orthodox leaders made haste to improve their triumph. The first step being over, confessions far more humiliating could now be extorted. Bonner came to his cell, and obtained from him a promise in writing, "to submit to the king and queen in all their laws and ordinances, as well touching the pope's supremacy, as in all other things;" with an engagement further "to move and stir all others to do the like," and to live in quietness and obedience, without murmur or grudging; his book on the sacrament he would submit to the next general council.

These three submissions must have followed one another rapidly. On the 16th of February, two days only after his trial, he made a fourth, and yielding the point which he had reserved, he declared that he believed all the articles of the Christian religion as the Catholic Church believed. But so far he had spoken generally, and the court required particulars. In a fifth and longer submission, he was made to anathematise particularly the heresies of Luther and Zuinglius; to accept the pope as the head of the church, out of which was no salvation; to acknowledge the real presence in the Eucharist, the seven sacraments as received by the Roman Catholics, and purgatory. He professed his penitence for having once held or taught otherwise, and he implored the prayers of all faithful Christians, that those whom he had seduced might be brought back to the true fold.

The demands of the church might have been satisfied by these last admissions; but Cranmer had not yet expiated his personal offences against the queen and her mother, and he was to drain the cup of humiliation to the dregs.

A month was allowed to pass. He was left with the certainty of his shame, and the uncertainty whether, after all, it had not been encountered in vain. On the 18th of March, one more paper was submitted to his signature, in which he confessed to be all which Pole had described him. He called himself a blasphemer, and a persecutor; being unable to undo his evil work, he had no hope, he said, save in the example of the thief upon the cross, who when other means of reparation were taken from him, made amends to God with his lips. He was unworthy of mercy, and he deserved eternal vengeance. He had sinned against King Henry and his wife; he was the cause of the divorce, from which, as from a seed, had sprung up schism, heresy, and crime; he had opened a window to false doctrines of which he had been himself the most pernicious teacher; especially he reflected with anguish that he had denied the presence of his Maker in the consecrated elements. He had deceived the living and he had robbed the souls of the dead by stealing from them their masses. He prayed the pope to pardon him; he prayed the king and queen to pardon him; he prayed God Almighty to pardon him, as he had pardoned Mary Magdalen; or to look upon him as, from his own cross, He had looked upon the thief.

The most ingenious malice could invent no deeper degradation, and the archbishop might now die. One favour was granted to him alone of all the sufferers for religion – that he might speak at his death; speak, and, like Northumberland, perish with a recantation on his lips.

The hatred against him was confined to the court. Even among those who had the deepest distaste for his opinions, his character had won affection and respect; and when it was known that he was to be executed, there was a widespread and profound emotion. "Although," says a Catholic who witnessed his death, "his former life and wretched end deserved a greater misery, if any greater might have chanced to him; yet, setting aside his offence to God and his country, beholding the man without his faults, I think there was none that pitied not his case and bewailed not his fortune, and feared not his own chance, to see so noble a prelate, so grave a councillor, of so long-continued honours, after so many dignities, in his old years to be deprived of his estate, adjudged to die, and in so painful a death to end his life."

On Saturday, the 21st of March, Lord Williams was again ordered into Oxford to keep the peace, with Lord Chandos, Sir Thomas Brydges, and other gentlemen of the county. If they allowed themselves to countenance by their presence the scene which they were about to witness, it is to be remembered that but a few years since, these same gentlemen had seen Catholic priests swinging from the pinnacles of their churches. The memory of the evil days was still recent, and amidst the tumult of conflicting passions, no one could trust his neighbour, and organised resistance was impracticable.

The March morning broke wild and stormy. The sermon intended to be preached at the stake was adjourned, in consequence of the wet, to St. Mary's, where a high stage was erected, on which Cranmer was to stand conspicuous. Peers, knights, doctors, students, priests, men-at-arms, and citizens, thronged the narrow aisles, and through the midst of them the archbishop was led in by the mayor. As he mounted the platform many of the spectators were in tears. He knelt and prayed silently, and Cole, the Provost of Eton, then took his place in the pulpit.

Although, by a strained interpretation of the law, it could be pretended that the time of grace had expired with the trial; yet, to put a man to death at all after recantation was a proceeding so violent and unusual, that some excuse or some explanation was felt to be necessary.

Cole therefore first declared why it was expedient that the late archbishop should suffer, notwithstanding his reconciliation. One reason was "for that he had been a great causer of all the alterations in the realm of England; and when the matter of the divorce between King Henry VIII and Queen Catherine was commenced in the court of Rome, he, having nothing to do with it, sate upon it as a judge, which was the entry to all the inconvenients which followed." "Yet in that Mr. Cole excused him – that he thought he did it, not out of malice, but by the persuasion and advice of certain learned men."

Another occasion was, "for that he had been the great setter-forth of all the heresy received into the church in the latter times; had written in it, had disputed, had continued it even to the last hour; and it had never been seen in the time of schism that any man continuing so long had been pardoned, and that it was not to be remitted for example's sake."

"And other causes," Cole added, "moved the queen and council thereto, which were not meet and convenient for every one to understand."

The explanations being finished, the preacher exhorted his audience to take example from the spectacle before them, to fear God, and to learn that there was no power against the Lord. There, in their presence, stood a man, once "of so high degree – sometime one of the chief prelates of the church – an archbishop, the chief of the council, the second person of the realm: of long time, it might be thought, in great assurance, a king on his side;" and now, "notwithstanding all his authority and defence, debased from a high estate unto a low degree – of a councillor become a caitiff, and set in so wretched estate that the poorest wretch would not change conditions with him."

Turning, in conclusion, to Cranmer himself, Cole then "comforted and encouraged him to take his death well by many places in Scripture; bidding him nothing mistrust but that he should incontinently receive that the thief did, to whom Christ said, To-day shalt thou be with me in Paradise. Out of Paul he armed him against the terrors of fire, by the words, The Lord is faithful, and will not suffer you to be tempted beyond that which you are able to bear; by the example of the three Children, to whom God made the flame seem like a pleasant joy; by the rejoicing of St. Andrew on his cross; by the patience of St. Lawrence on the fire." He dwelt upon his conversion, which, he said, was the special work of God, because so many efforts had been made by men to work upon him, and had been made in vain. God, in his own time, had reclaimed him, and brought him home.

A dirge, the preacher said, should be sung for him in every church in Oxford; he charged all the priests to say each a mass for the repose of his soul; and finally, he desired the congregation present to kneel where they were, and pray for him.

The whole crowd fell on their knees, the archbishop with them; and "I think," says the eye-witness, "that there was never such a number so earnestly praying together; for they that hated him before, now loved him for his conversion, and hopes of continuance: they that loved him before could not suddenly hate him, having hope of his confession; so love and hope increased devotion on every side."

"I shall not need," says the same writer, "to describe his behaviour for the time of sermon, his sorrowful countenance, his heavy cheer, his face bedewed with tears; sometimes lifting his eyes to heaven in hope, sometimes casting them down to the earth for shame – to be brief, an image of sorrow, the dolour of his heart bursting out of his eyes, retaining ever a quiet and grave behaviour, which increased the pity in men's hearts."

His own turn to speak was now come. When the prayer was finished, the preacher said, "Lest any man should doubt the sincerity of this man's repentance, you shall hear him speak before you. I pray you, Master Cranmer," he added, turning to him, "that you will now perform that you promised not long ago; that you would openly express the true and undoubted profession of your faith."

"I will do it," the archbishop answered.

"Good Christian people," he began, "my dear, beloved brethren and sisters in Christ, I beseech you most heartily to pray for me to Almighty God, that he will forgive me all my sins and offences, which be many and without number, and great above measure; one thing grieveth my conscience more than all the rest, whereof, God willing, I shall speak more; but how many or how great soever they be, I beseech you to pray God of his mercy to pardon and forgive them all."

Falling again on his knees:

"O Father of heaven," he prayed, "O Son of God, Redeemer of the world, O Holy Ghost, three Persons and one God, have mercy upon me, most wretched caitiff and miserable sinner. I have offended both heaven and earth more than my tongue can express; whither then may I go, or whither should I flee for succour? To heaven I am ashamed to lift up mine eyes, and in earth I find no succour nor refuge. What shall I do? Shall I despair? God forbid! Oh, good God, thou art merciful, and refusest none that come to thee for succour. To thee, therefore, do I come; to thee do I humble myself, saying, O Lord, my sins be great, yet have mercy on me for thy great mercy. The mystery was not wrought that God became man, for few or little offences. Thou didst not give thy Son, O Father, for small sins only, but for all and the greatest in the world, so that the sinner return to thee with a penitent heart, as I do at this present. Wherefore have mercy upon me, O Lord, whose property is always to have mercy; although my sins be great, yet is thy mercy greater; wherefore have mercy upon me, O Lord, for thy great mercy. I crave nothing, O Lord, for mine own merits, but for thy Name's sake, and, therefore, O Father of heaven, hallowed be thy Name."

Then rising, he went on with his address:

"Every man desireth, good people, at the time of his death, to give some good exhortation that others may remember after his death, and be the better thereby; for one word spoken of a man at his last end will be more remembered than the sermons made of them that live and remain. So I beseech God grant me grace, that I may speak something at my departing whereby God may be glorified and you edified.

"But it is an heavy case to see that many folks be so doted upon the love of this false world, and be so careful for it, that of the love of God or the world to come, they seem to care very little or nothing; therefore this shall be my first exhortation – that you set not over-much by this glozing world, but upon God and the world to come; and learn what this lesson meaneth which St. John teacheth, that the love of the world is hatred against God.

"The second exhortation is, that next unto God, you obey your king and queen willingly, without murmur or grudging, not for fear of them only, but much more for the fear of God, knowing that they be God's ministers, appointed of God to rule and govern you, and therefore whosoever resisteth them resisteth God's ordinance.

"The third exhortation is, that you live all together like brethren and sisters: but, alas! pity it is to see what contention and hatred one man hath against another, not taking each other for brethren and sisters, but rather as strangers and mortal enemies. But I pray you learn and bear well away the lesson, to do good to all men as much as in you lieth, and hurt no man no more than you would hurt your own natural brother or sister. For this you may be sure, that whosoever hateth his brother or sister, and goeth about maliciously to hinder or hurt him, surely, and without all doubt, God is not with that man, although he think himself never so much in God's favour.

"The fourth exhortation shall be to them that have great substance and riches of this world, that they may well consider and weigh these three sayings of the Scriptures. One is of our Saviour Christ himself, who saith that it is a hard thing for a rich man to come to heaven; a sore saying, and spoken of Him that knoweth the truth. The second is of St. John, whose saying is this: He that hath the substance of this world, and seeth his brother in necessity, and shutteth up his compassion and mercy from him, how can he say he loveth God? The third is of St. James, who speaketh to the covetous and rich men after this manner: Weep and howl for the misery which shall come upon you; your riches doth rot, your clothes be moth-eaten, your gold and silver is cankered and rusty, and the rust thereof shall bear witness against you, and consume you like fire; you gather and hoard up treasure of God's indignation against the last day. I tell them which be rich, ponder these sentences; for if ever they had occasion to show their charity, they have it now at this present; the poor people being so many, and victuals so dear; for although I have been long in prison, yet have I heard of the great penury of the poor."

The people listened breathless, "intending upon the conclusion."

"And now," he went on, "forasmuch as I am come to the last end of my life, whereupon hangeth all my life past and all my life to come, either to live with my Saviour Christ in joy, or else to be ever in pain with wicked devils in hell; and I see before mine eyes presently either heaven" – and he pointed upwards with his hand – "or hell," and he pointed downwards, "ready to swallow me. I shall therefore declare unto you my very faith, without colour or dissimulation; for now it is no time to dissemble. I believe in God the Father Almighty, Maker of heaven and earth; in every article of the Catholic faith; every word and sentence taught by our Saviour Christ, his apostles, and prophets, in the Old and New Testament.

"And now I come to the great thing that troubleth my conscience more than any other thing that ever I said or did in my life, and that is the setting abroad of writings contrary to the truth, which here I now renounce and refuse, as things written with my hand contrary to the truth which I thought in my heart, and written for fear of death to save my life, if it might be; and that is, all such bills and papers as I have written and signed with my hand since my degradation, wherein I have written many things untrue; and forasmuch as my hand offended in writing contrary to my heart, my hand therefore shall first be punished; for if I may come to the fire, it shall be the first burnt. As for the pope, I utterly refuse him, as Christ's enemy and Anti-Christ, with all his false doctrine; and as for the sacrament, I believe as I have taught in my book against the Bishop of Winchester."

So far the archbishop was allowed to continue, before his astonished hearers could collect themselves. "Play the Christian man," Lord Williams at length was able to call; "remember yourself; do not dissemble." "Alas! my lord," the archbishop answered, "I have been a man that all my life loved plainness, and never dissembled till now, which I am most sorry for." He would have gone on; but cries now rose on all sides, "Pull him down," "Stop his mouth," "Away with him," and he was borne off by the throng out of the church. The stake was a quarter of a mile distant, at the spot already consecrated by the deaths of Ridley and Latimer. Priest and monks "who did rue to see him go so wickedly to his death, ran after him, exhorting him, while time was, to remember himself." But Cranmer, having flung down the burden of his shame, had recovered his strength, and such words had no longer power to trouble him. He approached the stake with "a cheerful countenance," undressed in haste, and stood upright in his shirt. Soto and another Spanish friar continued expostulating; but finding they could effect nothing, one said in Latin to the other, "Let us go from him, for the devil is within him." An Oxford theologian – his name was Ely – being more clamorous, drew from him only the answer that, as touching his recantation, "he repented him right sore, because he knew that it was against the truth."

"Make short, make short!" Lord Williams cried, hastily.

The archbishop shook hands with his friends; Ely only drew back, calling, "Recant, recant," and bidding others not approach him.

"This was the hand that wrote it," Cranmer said, extending his right arm; "this was the hand that wrote it, therefore it shall suffer first punishment." Before his body was touched, he held the offending member steadily in the flame, "and never stirred nor cried." The wood was dry and mercifully laid; the fire was rapid at its work, and he was soon dead. "His friends," said a Catholic bystander, "sorrowed for love, his enemies for pity, strangers for a common kind of humanity, whereby we are bound to one another."

So perished Cranmer. He was brought out, with the eyes of his soul blinded, to make sport for his enemies, and in his death he brought upon them a wider destruction than he had effected by his teaching while alive. Pole was appointed the next day to the See of Canterbury; but in other respects the court had overreached themselves by their cruelty. Had they been contented to accept the recantation, they would have left the archbishop to die broken-hearted, pointed at by the finger of pitying scorn; and the Reformation would have been disgraced in its champion. They were tempted, by an evil spirit of revenge, into an act unsanctioned even by their own bloody laws; and they gave him an opportunity of redeeming his fame, and of writing his name in the roll of martyrs. The worth of a man must be measured by his life, not by his failure under a single and peculiar trial. The apostle, though forewarned, denied his Master on the first alarm of danger; yet that Master, who knew his nature in its strength and its infirmity, chose him for the rock on which He would build His church.

## THE END OF CATHOLIC ENGLAND

And these great events were now close, and the shadows were drawing down over the life of the unfortunate Mary. Amidst discontent and misery at home, disgrace and failure abroad, the fantastic comparisons, the delirious analogies, the child which was to be born of the Virgin Mary for the salvation of mankind – where were now these visionary and humiliating dreams?

On the 6th of October, the privy council were summoned to London "for great and urgent affairs." At the beginning of November three men and two women suffered at Canterbury. They were the last who were put to death, and had been presented by Pole in person to be visited "with condign punishment." On the 5th, parliament met, and the promised second subsidy was demanded, but the session was too brief for a resolution. The queen's life, at the time of the opening, was a question perhaps of hours, at most of days; and aware of what was impending, Philip despatched the Count de Feria to her with a desire that she should offer no objections to the succession of Elizabeth.

The count reached London on the 9th of November. He was admitted to an interview, and the queen, too brave to repine at what was now inevitable, and anxious to the last to please her husband, declared herself "well content" that it should be as he wished; she entreated only that her debts might be paid, and that "religion" should not be changed.

Leaving Mary's deathbed, De Feria informed the council of the king's request, and from the council hastened to the house of Lord Clinton, a few miles from London, where Elizabeth was staying. In Philip's name, he informed her that her succession was assured; his master had used his influence in her favour, and no opposition need be anticipated.

Elizabeth listened graciously. That Philip's services to her, however, had been so considerable as De Feria told her, she was unable to allow. She admitted, and admitted thankfully, the good offices which he had shown to her when she was at Woodstock. She was perhaps ignorant that it was for the safety of Philip's life that her own had been so nearly sacrificed; that Philip's interest in her succession had commenced only when his own appeared impossible. But she knew how narrow had been her escape; she had neither forgotten her danger, nor ceased to resent her treatment. It was to the people of England, she told the count, that she owed her real gratitude. The people had saved her from destruction; the people had prevented her sister from changing the settlement of the crown. She would be the people's queen, and she would reign in the people's interest.

De Feria feared, from what she said, that "in religion she would not go right." The ladies by whom she was surrounded were suspected; Sir William Cecil, whose conformity was as transparent then as it is now, would be her principal secretary; and the count observed, with a foreboding of evil, that "she had an admiration for the king her father's mode of ruling;" and that of the legate she spoke with cold severity.

It is possible that Pole was made acquainted with Elizabeth's feelings towards him. To himself personally, those feelings were of little moment, for he, too, like the queen, was dying – dying to be spared a second exile, and the wretchedness of seeing with his eyes the dissolution of the phantom fabric which he had given the labours of his life to build.

Yet what he did not live to behold he could not have failed to anticipate. The spirit of Henry VIII. was rising from the grave to scatter his work to all the winds; while he, the champion of Heaven, the destroyer of heresy, was lying himself under a charge of the same crime, with the pope for his accuser. Without straining too far the licence of imagination, we may believe that the disease which was destroying him was chiefly a broken heart. But it was painful to him to lie under the ill opinion of the person who was so soon to be on the throne of England; and possibly he wished to leave her, as a legacy, the warning entreaties of a dying man.

Three days after De Feria's visit, therefore, Pole sent the Dean of Worcester to Elizabeth with a message, the import of which is unknown; and a short letter, as the dean's credentials, saying only that the legate desired, before he should depart, to leave all persons satisfied of him, and especially her grace.

This was the 14th of November. The same day, or the day after, a lady-in-waiting carried the queen's last wishes to her successor. They were the same which she had already mentioned to De Feria – that her debts should be paid, and that the Catholic religion might be maintained, with an additional request that her servants should be properly cared for. Then, taking leave of a world in which she had played so ill a part, she prepared, with quiet piety, for the end. On the 16th, at midnight, she received the last rites of the church. Towards morning, as she was sinking, mass was said at her bedside. At the elevation of the Host, unable to speak or move, she fixed her eyes upon the body of her Lord; and as the last words of the benediction were uttered, her head sunk, and she was gone.

A few hours later (November 17), at Lambeth, Pole

followed her, and the reign of the pope of England, and the reign of terror, closed together.

No English sovereign ever ascended the throne with larger popularity than Mary Tudor. The country was eager to atone to her for her mother's injuries; and the instinctive loyalty of the English towards their natural sovereign was enhanced by the abortive efforts of Northumberland to rob her of her inheritance. She had reigned little more than five years, and she descended into the grave amidst curses deeper than the acclamations which had welcomed her accession. In that brief time she had swathed her name in the horrid epithet which will cling to it for ever; and yet from the passions which in general tempt sovereigns into crime, she was entirely free: to the time of her accession she had lived a blameless, and, in many respects, a noble life; and few men or women have lived less capable of doing knowingly a wrong thing.

Philip's conduct, which could not extinguish her passion for him, and the collapse of the inflated imaginations which had surrounded her supposed pregnancy, it can hardly be doubted, affected her sanity. Those forlorn hours when she would sit on the ground with her knees drawn to her face; those restless days and nights when, like a ghost, she would wander about the palace galleries, rousing herself only to write tear-blotted letters to her husband; those bursts of fury over the libels dropped in her way; or the marchings in procession behind the host in the London streets – these are all symptoms of hysterical derangement, and leave little room, as we think of her, for other feelings than pity. But if Mary was insane, the madness was of a kind which placed her absolutely under her spiritual directors; and the responsibility for her cruelties, if responsibility be anything but a name, rests first with Gardiner, who commenced them, and, secondly, and in a higher degree, with Reginald Pole. Because Pole, with the council, once interfered to prevent an imprudent massacre in Smithfield; because, being legate, he left the common duties of his diocese to subordinates, he is not to be held innocent of atrocities which could neither have been commenced nor continued without his sanction; and he was notoriously the one person in the council whom the queen absolutely trusted. The revenge of the clergy for their past humiliations, and the too natural tendency of an oppressed party to abuse suddenly recovered power, combined to originate the Marian persecution. The rebellions and massacres, the political scandals, the universal suffering throughout the country during Edward's minority, had created a general bitterness in all classes against the Reformers; the Catholics could appeal with justice to the apparent consequences of heretical opinions; and when the reforming preachers themselves denounced so loudly the irreligion which had attended their success, there was little wonder that the world took them at their word, and was ready to permit the use of strong suppressive measures to keep down the unruly tendencies of uncontrolled fanatics.

But neither these nor any other feelings of English growth could have produced the scenes which have stamped this unhappy reign with a character so frightful. The parliament which re-enacted the Lollard statutes, had refused to restore the Six Articles as being too severe; yet under the Six Articles twenty-one persons only suffered in six years; while, perhaps, not twice as many more had been executed under the earlier acts in the century and a half in which they had stood on the Statute roll. The harshness of the law confined the action of it to men who were definitely dangerous; and when the bishops' powers were given back to them, there was little anticipation of the manner in which those powers would be misused.

And that except from some special influences they would not have been thus misused, the local character of the persecution may be taken to prove. The storm was violent only in London, in Essex, which was in the diocese of London, and in Canterbury. It raged long after the death of Gardiner; and Gardiner, though he made the beginning, ceased after the first few months to take further part in it. The Bishop of Winchester would have had a persecution, and a keen one; but the fervour of others left his lagging zeal far behind. For the first and last time the true Ultramontane spirit was dominant in England; the genuine conviction that, as the orthodox prophets and sovereigns of Israel slew the worshippers of Baal, so were Catholics rulers called upon, as their first duty, to extirpate heretics as the enemies of God and man.

The language of the legate to the city of London shows the devout sincerity with which he held that opinion himself. Through him, and sustained by his authority, the queen held it; and by these two the ecclesiastical government of England was conducted.

Archbishop Parker, who succeeded Pole at Canterbury, and had therefore the best opportunity of knowing what his conduct had really been, called him *Carnifex et flagellum Ecclesæ Anglicanæ*, the hangman and the scourge of the Church of England. His character was irreproachable; in all the virtues of the Catholic Church he walked without spot or stain; and the system to which he had surrendered himself had left to him of the common selfishnesses of mankind his enormous vanity alone. But that system had extinguished also in him the human instincts, the genial emotions by which

164

theological theories stand especially in need to be corrected. He belonged to a class of persons at all times numerous, in whom enthusiasm takes the place of understanding; who are men of an "idea;" and unable to accept human things as they are, are passionate loyalists, passionate churchmen, passionate revolutionists, as the accidents of their age may determine. Happily for the welfare of mankind, persons so constituted rarely arrive at power: should power come to them, they use it, as Pole used it, to defeat the ends which are nearest to their hearts.

The teachers who finally converted the English nation to Protestantism were not the declaimers from the pulpit, nor the voluminous controversialists with the pen. These, indeed, could produce arguments which, to those who were already convinced, seemed as if they ought to produce conviction; but conviction did not follow till the fruits of the doctrine bore witness to the spirit from which it came. The evangelical teachers, caring only to be allowed to develop their own opinions, and persecute their opponents, had walked hand in hand with men who had spared neither tomb nor altar, who had stripped the lead from the church roofs, and stolen the bells from the church towers; and between them they had so outraged such plain honest minds as remained in England, that had Mary been content with mild repression, had she left the pope to those who loved him, and married, instead of Philip, some English lord, the mass would have retained its place, the clergy in moderate form would have resumed their old authority, and the Reformation would have waited for a century. In an evil hour, the queen listened to the unwise advisers, who told her that moderation in religion was the sin of the Laodicæans; and while the fanatics who had brought scandal on the Reforming cause, either truckled, like Shaxton, or stole abroad to wrangle over surplices and forms of prayer, the true and the good atoned with their lives for the crimes of others, and vindicated a noble cause by nobly dying for it.

And while among the Reformers that which was most bright and excellent shone out with preternatural lustre, so were the Catholics permitted to exhibit also the preternatural features of the creed which was expiring.

Although Pole and Mary could have laid their hands on earl and baron, knight and gentleman, whose heresy was notorious, although in the queen's own guard there were many who never listened to a mass, they dared not strike where there was danger that they would be struck in return. They went out into the highways and hedges; they gathered up the lame, the halt, and the blind; they took the weaver from his loom, the carpenter from his workshop, the husbandman from his plough; they laid hands on maidens and boys "who had never heard of any other religion than that which they were called on to abjure;" old men tottering into the grave, and children whose lips could but just lisp the articles of their creed; and of these they made their burnt-offerings; with these they crowded their prisons, and when filth and famine killed them, they flung them out to rot. How long England would have endured the repetition of the horrid spectacles is hard to say. The persecution lasted three years, and in that time something less than 300 persons were burnt at the stake. "By imprisonment," said Lord Burghley, "by torment, by famine, by fire, almost the number of 400 were," in their various ways, "lamentably destroyed."

Yet, as has been already said, interference was impossible except by armed force. The country knew from the first that by the course of nature the period of cruelty must be a brief one; it knew that a successful rebellion is at best a calamity; and the bravest and wisest men would not injure an illustrious cause by conduct less than worthy of it, so long as endurance was possible. They had saved Elizabeth's life and Elizabeth's rights, and Elizabeth, when her time came, would deliver her subjects. The Catholics, therefore, were permitted to continue their cruelties till the cup of iniquity was full; till they had taught the educated laity of England to regard them with horror; and till the Romanist superstition had died, amidst the execrations of the people, of its own excess.